LURE OF THE ARCTIC

(Lost on the Tundra)

By

Bernice M. Chappel

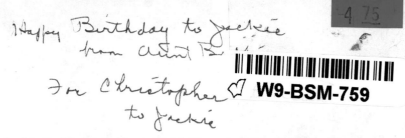

Drawings and Map

By

Marjorie Nash Klein

Also by Bernice M. Chappel

Listening and Learning

A Time for Learning

In the Palm of the Mitten

Bittersweet Trail

All characters in this novel
are fictitious. Any resemblance to
living persons, present or past, is coincidental.

LURE
OF THE
ARCTIC

———◆———

Bernice M. Chappel

Library of Congress Catalog Card Number: 86-50153

I S B N: C-9611596-2-6

Cover Photograph: "Travel Arctic"
Government of Northwest Territories

Typesetting by Thomas and Patricia Boufford
Okemos, Michigan

Published by:
Wilderness Adventure Books
320 Garden Lane
P. O. Box 968
Fowlerville, Michigan   48836

Manufactured in the United States of America

Dedicated to the Inuit,

the Eskimos of Northwest Territories.

ABOUT THE AUTHOR...

Bernice M. Chappel was associated with the field of education in Michigan for twenty-nine years. During this time she was a classroom teacher for nineteen years, followed by ten years as a school social worker. She holds a Bachelor of Science degree from Eastern Michigan University and a Master's degree in Education from the University of Michigan.

Since retirement she has had juvenile, teacher's aid, adult nonfiction and fiction books published. She is the author of:

Listening and Learning, a book designed
to develop listening skills in children

A Time for Learning, a self-instructional
handbook for parents and teachers

In the Palm of the Mitten, a memory book
of the author's early years in rural Michigan

Bittersweet Trail, a fictionalized historical
narrative of real people who lived in Michigan
in the 1800s.

Since her retirement, Bernice M. Chappel has visited nearly every country in North and Central America, several in South America, most of the Asian countries and a few European nations.
Lure of the Arctic was written after her interest in Eskimo culture was stimulated in 1975 by a visit to the Mackenzie River Delta area in Northwest Territories, Canada. Through her travels she gathers material and ideas for future books.

‘ᒪᓇ ᐃᓄᓯᑎᔭᒍᑦ, ᐅᒪᔪᕐ ᓯᐅᓂᖅ, ᓱᒐᓂᑎᓂ ᐊᓯᐅᓚᕐᒪᔭᖅ.
ᑕᒪᑯᐊ ᑕᐃᑦ ᓯᒪᓂᑕᐃᑦ ᐊᐅᓚᕈᔭᒍᑦ ᓄᐃᑕᒍᓇᐃᓚᕐᒪᔭᑦ.
ᑭᓯᐊᓂ ᐊᑦ ᓯᕿᓗᑕ ᐱᒪᓯᐊᑦ ᓯᐊᕿᑕ, ᐃᓕᓂᐊᑎᑦ ᓯᒪᓯᐊᕿᑕ
ᕿᑐᖅᕐᒪᑎᓂᒃ, ᐃᒪᖅ ᐳᐃᒍᓚᕐᒪᕐᒋᑲᓗᐊᖅ ᑐᒍᑦ.’

The way we live right now, by hunting, is going to be lost in the future. The memories of the past are going to disappear. But if we try hard enough, if we try to teach our children, I hope maybe we are not going to forget.

— *Stephen Guion Williams,* ***In the Middle***

CONTENTS

Chapter   Page

1   Adventure Beckons   1

2   Tuktoyaktuk   23

3   The Boat Trip to Kendall Island   59

4   Whale Camp   103

5   Aklavik   154

6   Survival   178

7   The Relentless Arctic   219

8   The End of an Adventure   237

       Glossary   258

       Bibliography   261

MAP OF AREA

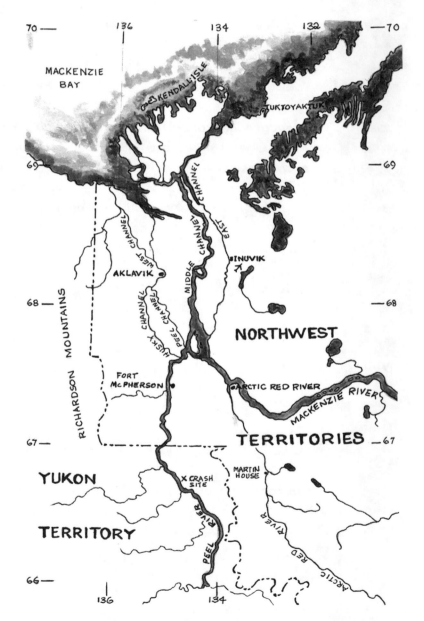

ACKNOWLEDGMENTS

This book, **Lure of the Arctic,** became a reality because of the cooperation and hard work of the following people:

Special thanks to Clayton Klein, author of **Cold Summer Wind** and **One Incredible Journey,** for his suggestions and for sharing his knowledge of Canada's Northwest Territories.

Special thanks to Marjorie Nash Klein for her assistance in preparing the maps and for her interpretation of the incidents in the book through her fine illustrations.

Special thanks to Ann Taylor, former editor of **COPE** (Committee for Original Peoples' Entitlement) for supplying information about the Mackenzie River Delta area.

Thanks to Father Guy Mary-Rousselière, o.m.i., editor of **Eskimo,** and to Father Etienne Bazin, o.m.i., for their fine photos of the Inuit.

Thanks to Agnes Semmler of Inuvik and David McNeill, editor of **Tusaayaksat,** for their interest.

Thanks to Tom and Pat Boufford of Word Processing Services of Okemos, Michigan, for their assistance in helping to produce **Lure of the Arctic.**

ADVENTURE   BECKONS

The Boeing 737 slid through the evening skies
toward Inuvik, Northwest Territories, Canada. Paul
Douglas squinted into the sun. "For a time in the
northern part of the Northwest Territories, the sun
doesn't set at all," he remarked.

"Yep." His father, a fortyish, athletic appearing six-footer idly flipped the pages of the latest
newsmagazine.

Paul continued. "After we find work I hope
there'll be time to get acquainted with some of the
Eskimo people. I'd like to know more about the way
they live. One of my sociology assignments this
fall at the university will be to interpret the culture of a minority group."

LURE OF THE ARCTIC

Jim Douglas closed the magazine. "Have you definitely decided to major in social work? There are other fields that pay better."

Paul nodded. "Money isn't everything, Dad. I like people. Maybe, with training, I can help some of my troubled peers to solve their problems."

"You mean the drug thing?"

"That's part of it." He was silent a moment. "Carl says I'm stupid for going into social work. He thinks I should be an engineer like he is. I'm glad to get away this summer. Carl and I don't hit it off too well."

"Your stepfather means well. What does your mother say about it?"

"She thinks I should — " The captain's voice came over the loud speaker. "We're flying at an altitude of 35,000 feet. We'll land at Norman Wells at 10:30. The weather there is clear and the temperature is forty degrees Fahrenheit or five degrees Celsius."

Jim cleared his throat. "You've never liked Carl. Why?"

"Well — I'm grown now, but some of the feelings I had when Mom married him are still there. He took your place. That hurt." He paused, then added impulsively, "I'm glad you asked me to go with you this summer."

Jim was silent. Finally he said, "Carl should have been a good model for you as a child. He's steady and reliable."

"And boring!"

"I hope you don't follow my example, Paul. I use poor judgment. I'm too impulsive — that's what your mother always said, and she's right. Like this trip — I don't know if we can find work in Inuvik. We have our return tickets, but there's not much cash for food and lodging. We'd better find something soon."

For a time they were silent, deep in thought. Paul stared into the fleecy white clouds. They reminded him of fluffy snowbanks. After a time he asked, "How far is it to Inuvik?"

"About thirty-three hundred miles by air from Toronto."

The captain's voice announced, "We'll sit down for fifteen minutes in the petroleum producing area of Norman Wells. As we descend you will see the Mackenzie River on the left. The Mackenzie is the largest river in Canada. It flows north and west for twelve hundred miles from Great Slave Lake to the Beaufort Sea, which is part of the Arctic Ocean."

The lighted sign, "Fasten Seat Belts" flashed on at the front of the cabin. The click of locking buckles could be heard as the stewardess walked down the aisle visually checking the seat belt of each passenger.

The plane broke through the clouds into bright sunlight. "There's the Mackenzie, Dad!" Paul exclaimed. "There are boats on it."

"Those four barges are being pushed by a diesel tug. They take supplies to the northern settlements after the ice goes out of the river near the end of May. Maybe we can get work unloading freight at Inuvik."

The plane touched down at the Norman Wells airport. Two men got off. A truck backed up to the cargo section and a crane swung several large crates from the plane to the truck. A few minutes later the 737 again was airborne. Soon the captain announced, "We'll arrive in Inuvik in forty-five minutes."

Paul glanced at his watch. "It's 10:45 at night but it's as light as the middle of the afternoon at home."

In a short time the 737 glided to a stop on the runway of the modern Inuvik airport. Planes of various makes and sizes were parked on the ramp and just off the edges of the runway.

Jim and Paul, with the other passengers, went inside to wait for their luggage. A yellow bus, which reminded Paul of a school bus, waited to take the passengers to Inuvik eight and one-half miles to the northwest. From snatches of conversation which they overheard Paul and Jim decided that most of the passengers were part of a tour group.

In the bus Jim spoke to a white-haired man across the aisle. "Where are you staying?"

"At the Eskimo Inn. And you?"

"We don't have reservations. We might try the

Eskimo Inn too."

The bus jolted along the dusty dirt road. The dark-skinned bus driver picked up the microphone. "You have noticed our dust." He turned on the bus lights and edged far to the right of the road. "We have very little rain here. In fact, this area is almost a desert. You may be surprised to see forests of spruce, birch and willow in the Arctic. Inuvik is near the border of the tree line. There are few trees on the tundra north of Inuvik." He stopped talking as the headlights of an approaching vehicle glowed dimly through the haze of dust.

Paul whispered to his father. "Is the driver Eskimo or Indian?"

"Probably Eskimo."

Paul absently traced his initials in the dust which already lay thick on his brown suitcase. The driver went on. "You are wondering why we don't pave this road. In the Arctic the permafrost is a thousand feet thick. In summer the frost goes out in the top two or three feet. We live with a lot of mud and dust." He paused. "We have only a few miles of road outside Inuvik. Right now you can reach our town only by way of the Mackenzie River or by air. But when the Dempster Highway is completed cars and trucks will travel the entire distance to Inuvik from the United States and Canada." Paul stared at the scrubby dust-laden trees which were only about twenty feet high.

The driver continued. "Along the roadside,

notice the rose-purplish plant which is starting to bloom. It is fireweed and it grows all over the Arctic." He stared intently into an impenetrable cloud of dust left from a truck they had met. "We're coming into town now. Inuvik is a fairly new community that started from scratch in the late 1950s. It was incorporated as a village eight years ago in 1967. New housing ideas are tried here. The buildings are painted bright colors ranging from yellow through blue and green to deep shades of rust and brown." He turned toward the passengers. "Did you ever see a town with so many bright-colored homes and apartment houses?"

"No, but it looks nice," a woman said.

"This part of Inuvik, the east end, is where most of the government workers live." He motioned toward the brightly painted federal apartments. "Native Eskimo and Indian families live in the west end of the city. Our population is a little over three thousand. Many people here are oil workers, and most of the others are employed by the government, and some also work on the docks in summer. Everything we have is brought in by plane or ship for nothing is produced here," he smiled, "that is, except little Eskimos and Indians."

The passengers chuckled. In a moment he went on. "A few native families still hunt and have trap lines in winter. Among the native settlements of the western Arctic, Inuvik is the 'head office.' We have the continent's northernmost CBC television and radio stations, a large Eskimo-Indian hospital and school, and the headquarters for the Royal Canadian Police and for barge and ship operators. All of these as well as the game management and regional administrators for Northwest Territories are located here. You can see why Inuvik is a 'government city'."

The bus stopped before the Eskimo Inn which was a white two-story building with orange and blue native symbols of a smiling sun on the front. A few pickup trucks and cars were parked on either side of the long flight of metal steps which led to the lobby of the Inn. Scraps of paper and discarded cans littered the edges of the rutted dusty street. Paul and Jim hurried up the steps as the tour group slowly left the bus.

They registered at the desk, taking a single room because it was less expensive than a double. The clerk gave them a key. "Your room is up this flight of stairs," he motioned, "and then to the left." He smiled. "You'll enjoy our TV."

"I didn't think you'd have TV 'way up here," Paul said.

The man nodded. "Our government put up a satellite and we have fine reception. It has made a big difference in the lives of our people. We also can telephone anywhere in the world via the satellite. There's not much to do here except to work. We have a motion picture theater and our churches provide some recreation, but there's only a few miles of road outside of town. It will be different when the Dempster Highway is completed for we'll be able to travel south to other settlements." He glanced at the group of people coming toward the desk. "Enjoy your stay in Inuvik." He turned toward the tour director.

As they entered their room the sun shone through the open drapery of the west window. Paul looked out. "We are on the back of the hotel," he said. "There are lots of young kids out there and it's 12:30 at night. Hey, Dad! Come here!"

Jim came to the window. Paul pointed. "What are those big metal tubes that run into the back of the buildings? And there are steps so that people can get over them. They must be more than seven feet high."

"Hm-m-m. I don't know what they are. And have you noticed that most of the buildings are built on pilings?"

"Yeah. They're on stilts."

Jim turned away. "Let's get to bed and tomorrow we'll explore Inuvik and try to find work."

The next morning they were in the coffee shop by seven o'clock. They searched the menu. Finally Paul muttered, "They don't have cereal."

A man sitting next to him at the counter said, "Can't get fresh milk. It will be different when the Dempster Highway is finished. We'll have fresh milk, vegetables and many things we do without now."

"We hadn't thought of that," Jim said. "So most

of your fruits and vegetables are canned?"

"That's right. Where are you from?"

"I'm from Toronto and my son lives in Detroit."

"I see. I'm from Vancouver. I'm an oil worker."

The waitress took their order and the conversation continued. "I like it here," the man went on. "I make good money and since I don't have a family, this is as good a place as any."

"Are they hiring in the oil industry?" Jim asked.

"No. The environmentalists are putting up a fight, and the native people say the land originally belonged to them and they've been negotiating claims with the government, so right now not many new projects are being started."

"We'd like to find work for the summer," Jim said. "Do you have any suggestions?"

"You might try the docks. It's hard work and long hours but it pays well."

Paul piled strawberry jam on his piece of toast. "What are those huge metal pipes behind the buildings?"

"That's the utilidor. It's an above-ground system that carries water, sewers, heating pipes and electricity."

"You can't put any pipes underground?"

"No, because of the permafrost. It's a thousand feet deep. It's impossible to get below the frost line, so the solution was utilidors. They are box-like insulated containers that are built on pilings above the ground. There are both hot and cold water

pipes in the utilidors. The warm water also heats the buildings so that people who use the utilidor don't have furnaces or chimneys."

"That's neat. Do all of the people use the utilidor?"

"No. Many of the homes in the native section heat with fuel oil or bottled gas, and their garbage and sewage is picked up each week by truck."

LURE OF THE ARCTIC

Later, wearing jackets and gloves, Jim and Paul went out into a damp, misty morning. A brightly painted one-story building was directly across from the Inn. "That is the Hudson's Bay Company store, and the blue building to the left is the Centennial Library." Jim absently lighted a cigarette as he studied the signs.

"There's a drug store and a men's clothing store, but there aren't many business places," Paul observed. "Hey! There is the Royal Canadian Mounted Police headquarters!"

Their footsteps made a hollow sound on the wooden walks. Paul remarked, "The walks must be built on top of the ground because of the permafrost."

"Yeah. I expect this place is a sea of mud in the spring."

Paul pulled his hood over his head. Two teenage boys smiled as they approached them. "Hi!" he said.

"Hi!" they answered.

Jim asked, "Are we going the right way to the docks?"

One of the youths motioned. "They're over that way. Want us to show you?"

"Do you have time?" Paul grinned.

"Sure," the taller boy said.

"My name is Paul Douglas, and this is my father, Jim," Paul said.

"Hi. We're brothers. I'm Morris Katoayak and this is Billy. Our father works at the docks in summer."

11

"What does he do in winter?" Jim asked.

"He has a trapline."

"Does he have a dog team?" Paul asked.

Morris shook his head. "Hardly anyone uses dog teams now. He has a Skidoo."

"Our father likes the snowmobile because he says he doesn't have to hunt and fish to feed it like you do with dogs," Billy laughed.

"What animals does he trap?" Jim asked.

"Mostly muskrats, but also ermine, martens, foxes, rabbits, wolves and a few beaver. Then he hunts caribou, moose, ducks and swans for food," Morris answered.

"It sounds exciting," Paul said.

"We like our life. We wouldn't want to live in a big city," Billy said. "Our father says it's not the same around here since the government built Inuvik. He used to live in Aklavik when he was little. My grandparents still live there."

"Where's Aklavik?"

"Thirty-five miles across the Mackenzie Delta west of here. It's an old town, not new like Inuvik."

Paul studied a building in the distance. "What's that building that looks like a big igloo?"

"That's our igloo church. It's made of cement blocks, but it looks like an igloo if you're not too close," Morris said. "Our family goes to church there. Our priest sometimes makes beautiful ice sculptures in winter. Last year he made a big

sculpture of Mary and the baby Jesus.   The church is
real pretty inside."

"Do you live in Inuvik in winter or do you live
near your father's trap line?" Paul asked.

Morris said, "We live here."

"Do any of the people live on the tundra in snow
houses in winter?"

"No.   If a trapper gets lost in bad weather, or

if he has trouble with his snowmobile he would make a little shelter from snow and canvass — if the snow conditions were right."

Paul's eyes showed his interest. "Do you know how to make a snow house?"

Morris shook his head. "The Delta Inuit didn't build snow houses often. We didn't need to because we have driftwood logs that come down the Mackenzie. Our people, in the old days, used to build log cabins, or they would put up tents and block them with snow for insulation."

"Hm-m-m," Paul mused. "I thought all Eskimos used to live in snow houses in winter."

Morris explained. "The Inuit in Northwest Territories east of the Delta built snow houses — that was because they didn't have any wood."

"How cold does it get here?" Jim asked.

"Last year it was seventy degrees below zero one morning."

"Wow! How do you stand it?" Paul exclaimed. "Does your father's Skidoo ever stop so he has to make a shelter to keep from freezing?"

Billy shook his head. "He takes good care of his Skidoo so it won't stop. We know an Inuit trapper who has both a snowmobile and a dog team. He pulls the dogs behind the Skidoo on a sled. Then if he has trouble, the dogs will get him home. It looks funny. His dogs sit on the sled behind the Skidoo and they hold their heads high. They look as though they're saying, 'Look at us. We've got it made'."

Jim laughed. "That man believes in being prepared."

As they walked along Paul said, "Why are the buildings on stilts?"

Morris seemed puzzled. "Stilts?"

Paul laughed. "Pilings. They remind me of stilts that I walked on when I was a kid."

"I see what you mean." They stopped at a corner where many evenly spaced posts protruded from four to six feet above the ground. Morris went on, "Next year there will be a recreation hall built here. The posts were driven into the permafrost last week. Next winter it will freeze around them. When summer comes again the posts will be cut off four or five feet above the ground. They will make a solid platform for the new building."

"Don't you have basements?"

Morris shook his head. "I've never seen a basement. No one has them in the Arctic. The permafrost would thaw around them and under them and the building would sink and get uneven."

The cold gray fog was heavy as they approached the river. "Do you have much fog?" Jim asked.

"We do in June, but fog can move in anytime. Sometimes it lasts a day or two. Usually there are planes coming and going, but they don't fly much in the fog," Morris said.

Activity increased as they approached the river. Trucks and tractors with fork lifts maneuvered as they moved the heavy boxes to the dock. Several red mobile homes had recently been unloaded. Great piles of heavy crates were stacked like building blocks. Men with hard hats were everywhere, each one intent on his work.

Billy exclaimed, "Look Morris! There's our new fire truck! They've just unloaded it!" The brightly painted truck had "Inuvik Fire Department" in large block letters on the side.

"Yeah." His eyes searched the dock. In a moment he said, "There's our father. He's the one in the orange hard hat. He is talking to Pete." The man began moving crates to another location. "I guess Dad told him he'd put the crates in the wrong place.

Our father is a foreman," he explained.

Paul's eyes met his father's. In a few minutes the boys' father came toward them. "No baseball today?" he asked. The boys shook their heads.

Morris said, "Dad, this is Jim Douglas and his son, Paul."

The short-legged, stocky man held out his hand. "Nice to meet you. I'm Joe Katoayak. Are you going to be in Inuvik long?"

"That depends," Jim answered. "My son and I are from Toronto and Detroit. We want to see the Arctic and stay for the summer if we can find work. Would there be anything open with your group?"

Joe shook his head. "We're filled up. I've got a good gang this year. They're hard workers who are glad for seven days work a week. Sometimes we get a man who wants part time work. We let him go because we have only a few weeks to get in the yearly supplies for the settlements. The twelve to fourteen weeks go by fast, for the ice goes out of the river in June and forms again in early October. It's a constant race against the freeze-up."

"Would you have an idea where we might find work?" Jim asked.

"Not in Inuvik. I have a brother, Jack Katoayak, who is a foreman on the docks at Tuktoyaktuk. He didn't have a full crew a few days ago."

"Where is that place, Tukto — ? I can't say it." Jim laughed.

"It's a jawbreaker for new people. Tuktoyaktuk.

LURE OF THE ARCTIC

It's about seventy miles north on the Beaufort Sea. The Northern Transportation Company there transfers freight from the MacKenzie River barges to ocean vessels which take it to settlements in the Arctic."

"And you think we might get work there?"

"There's a chance." Joe scribbled his brother's name and a phone number on a piece of paper and gave it to Jim. "You might call Jack. Tell him you talked with me. That phone number is at the docks, so you can reach Jack there most any time. I hope you find work." He turned to Morris and Billy. "See you tonight."

Jim thanked the boys' father who went back to his crew. For a time they watched as men unloaded, sorted and piled materials which had been ordered by Inuvik business people and private citizens. Piles of dry goods enclosed in water-repellent, air-tight plastic cocoons, pre-fabricated sections of houses, mobile homes, plastic cisterns and pieces of drilling pipe, all were piled on the dock.

"It's hard to realize that 'most everything here is brought in by water or air," Jim said.

"Yeah," Paul mused, "there are no roads or railroads to transport things."

"We're used to it," Billy said. "It costs so much to ship by air that people try to use water transportation."

"Even our petroleum comes by barge. Some of our gasoline and heating oil and aviation fuel is down in the hold of that orange-colored barge." Morris pointed.

"I thought you had oil wells," Paul said.

"We do, but oil's not refined here."

"Hm-m-m. You have lots of petroleum, but it has to be shipped out, refined, and shipped back to you," Paul said.

On the way back to the Eskimo Inn Billy and Morris took them past the Sir Alexander Mackenzie High School which both boys attended. The modern two-story building, like others in Inuvik, was built on pilings about three feet above the ground.

"We are lucky," Morris said. "We can live at home and go to school. Children in some of the settlements go to grade nine at home and after that they live at the hostel. They don't get home often, sometimes only when school is out in the summer."

Morris continued. "Next year my cousin Margaret Katoayak will come here to school. She'll live with us."

"Where does she live?"

"At Tuk."

"Where's Tuk?"

Morris laughed. "That's short for Tuktoyaktuk. Margaret's father, our Uncle Jack, is the man you're going to call about work, Mr. Douglas."

Jim glanced at his watch. "I'd like to get back to the hotel and make that call."

They parted at the Eskimo Inn and the brothers started toward the native section of town. "Thanks for going with us to the docks," Jim said, "and for telling us about Inuvik."

"Maybe we'll see you again!" Paul called.

The boys waved and went on past the log fur shop and native handicraft store beside the Inn.

While Jim made the phone call, Paul went to their room to watch a TV program about Eskimo whale hunting in Kugmallit Bay near Tuktoyaktuk. The way of life of the Arctic people seemed strange and exciting.

Jim was whistling as he opened the door. "How would you like to live in Tuktoyaktuk this summer?" he shouted.

"Dad! You found work for us?"

Jim closed the door. "Not for sure, but Jack Katoayak says they need another man and I have an appointment to see him as soon as we can get to Tuk. I didn't push my luck and ask for both of us."

"How do we get there?"

"By charter plane. I called and we can get a pilot with a small plane tomorrow morning if the weather is good."

"Is it expensive?"

"Yes, but if I land this job we'll be all set. Dock workers have long hours, but they're well paid. Of course, everything is expensive here. Food, lodging, clothing — you pay plenty for anything you get." He paused. "I'm hoping there will be work for you at the docks too."

At noon they studied the menu in the dining room of the Inn. Jim said, "Let's have something differ-

Inuvik apartment house on pilings

ent."

"Okay.   What'll we have?"

"Caribou steak."

When their orders came they found the large steak with potatoes and peas to be excellent.   "It tastes a little like beef, and a little like venison," Jim said.

The rest of the day they spent going through the few stores and walking in the native section of town.   The small brightly painted houses were a contrast to the neat apartment houses and private homes of the East End. Beside most of the native houses was a pickup truck or an old Volkswagen. A rusty fuel oil tank on a rickety platform sat by the front doors. One or two barking dogs were tied in the yards or on the porches. No grass grew in the lawns but clumps of fireweed blossomed here and there. A rusty barrel which served as a trash burner sat in front of each house near the street. All of the homes had a snowmobile parked near the house, and some had two or three.

The people they met nodded or spoke. "I like these people," Paul said. "If we stay at Tuk I hope we can find friends there."

2

TUKTOYAKTUK

The next day fog prevented air traffic until one o'clock in the afternoon.   The bush pilot, Walter Maniksak, a cigarette hanging from his mouth, stooped to fold his rubber boots another turn. Then, stuffing his blue jeans inside them, he straightened and brushed back his heavy black hair. Turning to Paul and Jim he said, "Climb in and I'll load your luggage."

When they were loaded the pilot of the single engine four passenger Cessna 185 took a last puff on his cigarette before he flipped it away.   He climbed in and closed the door.   The motor started with a roar.   As it warmed up Walter removed his plaid jacket and threw it to the right on the floor.

Adjusting his headphones, he listened as directions were given from the control tower. After a few words of reply, they taxied down the runway and shortly were airborne.

Below them was Inuvik. There was the Eskimo Inn, the barges on the river, the docks, the igloo church and the brightly colored buildings with the utilidor snaking behind them. An occasional car or truck stirred up clouds of dust as they traveled the road to the airport.

The steady roar of the motor made conversation difficult. Flying north, they passed the tree line. The Mackenzie twisted and turned on its way to the Arctic Ocean. On both sides of the plane as far as the eye could see there was water, ponds, lakes and small streams dotting the brownish-green tundra. Below was a filigree of water and land so inter-meshed that it was difficult to know whether they were crossing a vast lake filled with innumerable islands or a vast land clotted with innumerable lakes. As the last ghostly layers and wisps of ground fog drifted away, a haze lay over the tundra, even in the sunlight. There were no signs of life, either human or animal.

Paul wondered what they would do if there was trouble with the plane. There was no place to land, and probably the tundra was too wet for plane wheels. He put the thought from his mind and con-centrated on the watery scene below. He wondered how far the tundra went. This land and water were part of the Mackenzie Delta and he knew it was large. Suddenly he saw something — a strange appearing building. He nudged his father and pointed. "Oil well," Jim shouted close to Paul's ear.

He returned to his thoughts. Could anyone walk down there between the ponds, lakes and streams? From the air it was a pretty combination of colors. In some places the tundra was brown, other areas were reddish-brown, while still others were various shades of green.

After about an hour Paul noticed three rounded hills on the horizon. They reminded him of pimples on the flat face of the tundra. He pointed. Jim shrugged that he didn't know what they were.

The pilot spoke into his mike. He spoke again. For the next few minutes he worked and fussed with the radio. Finally he gave up. Paul looked at his father questioningly. Jim shrugged. Soon they were within sight of a village on the shore of a vast body of water that was the Beaufort Sea, a part of the Arctic Ocean.

Jim pointed to a radar base with its huge reflectors. "Distant Early Warning base," he shouted. "The DEW Line!"

They circled the village coming in low over the gravel runway. The wheels touched down and they rolled to a stop. The pilot turned off the engine, removed his headphones and unfastened the seat belt. "Welcome to Tuktoyaktuk!" he said.

"You had trouble with the radio?" Paul asked.

"I have a little problem with it now and then. I'll have to get it fixed." He moved the luggage away from the plane a short distance. "After I get the plane off the runway, I'll call Sam to pick us up. Guess you want to stay at the Lodge — that's the only place that has rooms and board in Tuk."

"Then the Lodge it is," Jim laughed.

Paul shaded his eyes and looked to the southwest. "What are those little hills we flew over? There's one out there." He pointed.

The pilot set the luggage near the small terminal. "Pingos. They're hills of ice. Tuktoyaktuk is one of the few areas where there are pingos."

"What causes them?"

"There's lots of silt — fine grained soil — in tundra lakes. As the lake fills with silt, the permafrost gradually freezes it around the sides of the lakes. Finally the silt becomes frozen to the center and because the water can't expand sideways, it bulges up as it freezes and over many years it forms that ice-covered hill you see."

"Would it be possible to walk to that pingo?"

"It's hard going. Mud, water, muskeg and mosquitoes. There's a pingo here in the village." The pilot went inside the terminal. When he came back he said, "Sam Rubin runs the only taxi in Tuk. He's not very busy," he smiled, "so he'll be here in about five minutes."

Jim inquired, "Are you going back to Inuvik?"

"Not tonight. I'll stay with my parents."

LURE OF THE ARCTIC

Climbing into the plane Walter taxied it off the runway, got out and locked the door.

An old car rattled and shook along the bumpy dusty road toward the airport. The driver jumped out. "Hi, Walter!" He turned to Jim. "You want to go to the Lodge?"

"We do." Jim and Paul put their suitcases in the back and climbed in. Walter sat in front with Sam.

Children and dogs romped in the dusty street. There were few cars. The houses were small, some made of logs and others had painted wooden or aluminum siding. Old men sitting on the steps in the cool June sunshine waved at Sam and Walter.

Soon they stopped before a log building which stood a short distance from the shore of the Beaufort Sea. Jim paid the taxi fare and turned toward the Lodge.

A rustic sign with the words "The Lodge" hung above the railing-enclosed, eight foot wooden porch. A second door with a set of moose antlers above it opened into a wing at the left.

Hesitating, Jim said, "Let's leave our luggage here." They went inside. The room seemed to be a living room. Two couches with matching chairs, a small table and an oil heater occupied most of the space. Paul pulled back the bright print drapes. "There's the DEW Line base across the water."

Jim nodded. "Let's try the other door." They went outside and up two wooden steps into a room with red and white oilcloth-covered tables and a counter with bar stools before it. The spicy aroma of gingerbread filled the air and a kettle simmered on the bottled gas range. The clatter of a typewriter came from a room at the right.

"Hi!" A woman called as she came through the door at the rear of the room. "You're strangers to Tuk. Can I help you?"

"We would like a room."

A little girl carrying a doll came to stand behind her mother. "Fine. We don't have any guests yet. We're just opening for the summer, so you have the choice of any of our seven rooms. How long will you be staying?" She brushed back her shoulder length hair.

"We hope to get work at the docks. If we do, we'll stay for the summer. Can we get our meals here?"

"Sure thing. I'll show you the room." She led the way to the living room wing. "There are three rooms and a bathroom besides the living room in this part of the lodge. You might prefer a room here. My husband types — he's a writer — and this wing is more quiet. You're welcome to use the living room."

They chose a room with a double bed and two windows overlooking the Arctic Ocean. After they agreed on the price for meals and lodging, the woman said, "I like the view from this room, too. We love Tuk. Our home is in Montreal. My husband is a teacher but we come here in summer to manage the Lodge. Peter has time to write and the Lodge doesn't have so many guests that the work is hard for me."

Paul carried in the suitcases. The woman turned. "Before you unpack, come to the dining room and have some fresh gingerbread."

The little girl smiled shyly at Paul. "Hi," he said. "What is your name?"

"Michele LeBeau." She hid behind her mother.

Later as they sat at the counter, the clatter of the typewriter stopped and a tall, bearded man came into the dining room.

"Peter," the woman said, "these are our first guests — " she hesitated.

"Jim and Paul Douglas," Jim volunteered.

"I'm Peter LeBeau, and you've already met Marie and Michele."

After a short time Jim glanced at his watch. "It's 4:30 Paul. Let's go see about those jobs."

Peter directed them and they hurried down the narrow dirt street toward the harbor, observing the homes as they walked. "Dad," Paul said, "what is hanging on the line beside that cabin?"

"Looks like skins of some kind."

"They're from a good sized animal."

"They look like deer hides."

"I know, Dad. Remember Morris and Billy said their father hunts caribou? I'll bet they're caribou hides."

"You're probably right. We have a lot to learn about this country."

LURE OF THE ARCTIC

Small children playing beside houses and in the street stared as they passed. Dogs ran barking until someone called them off. Paul watched for young men near his age but he saw only younger children, women and a few old men. The children were dressed as those at home would be on a chilly spring day.

The young women wore jeans and jackets, while the older ladies had on light-weight hooded parka type garments that fell below the knees. Most of them had slacks under the parkas and some wore heavy winter boots.

Soon they arrived at the docks. The activity and operations they had seen at Inuvik were repeated at Tuk. The employees were hard at work. Jim approached a man who was piling crates. "Can you tell us where we can find Jack Katoayak?"

The man hesitated briefly while he glanced about. "He's talking to the truck driver. He has on an orange jacket and a white hard hat." The man returned to his work.

"Thanks." They wandered toward a ship in the harbor. Workers were transferring cargo from the dock to the large steamship. The crates and boxes were marked for delivery at Coppermine, N.W.T.

Paul walked about the dock reading addresses on other cargo. Large piles were marked for Sachs Harbor, Cambridge Bay, Gjoa Haven and Spence Bay. Suddenly he felt that someone was watching him. He turned. His father was talking to a man nearby.

"Hi!" A stocky young man called.

"Hi! I was looking at some of the places this cargo is going. Sachs Harbor, Cambridge Bay, Gjoa Haven, Spence Bay and Coppermine. Where are those places?"

"Sachs Harbor is north and east of Tuk on Banks Island. The others are mostly east, but they're all in Northwest Territories."

"The Northwest Territories is a big area."

"It goes across northern Canada from the Yukon to the Atlantic Ocean."

Paul grinned. "Yeah, that's big." Silently he wondered about the young man. Was he Eskimo or Indian? How old was he? What was his life like?

The man asked, "Are you visiting Tuk?"

"Yes. My father is talking to Mr. Katoayak about our getting work here."

The young man smiled broadly. "Jack Katoayak is my father. Mother sent a lunch to him because he will work late." He held up a brown bag. "He wants to finish loading this ship tonight."

"I'm Paul Douglas from Detroit, Michigan, U.S.A."

"Yes. The place where they make automobiles. And I'm John Katoayak, Jr. I hope Dad still has spots for both of you. We could do things together. I've never had a friend from the U.S.A."

"I'd like that too. I know your cousins in Inuvik."

"Morris and Billy? We don't see them very often since I graduated from high school. Next year I have a sister who'll live with them while she's in high school."

"Morris and Billy told me." He looked up. "My father's coming."

Jim called, "I'm going to start work now, but there was only one opening. Perhaps you can find something else."

Disappointed, Paul stared at the ground. John turned to leave. "I'm working at the general store days until five, but maybe I'll see you some night after work, Paul."

"Sure thing." Paul turned to his father. "Maybe Mrs. LeBeau will put up a lunch for you, Dad. I'll bring it back."

"Good. I don't know when I'll be through work.

Don't wait up for me."

The next morning Paul ate an early breakfast with his father and Jim explained his hours. "We work seven days a week, and sometimes I'll put in eighteen hour days." He paused. "Did you line up a job?"

"I talked with Mrs. LeBeau. She wasn't very encouraging — said there's not much work here except at the docks. I asked at all the stores, but there's nothing." Paul slowly buttered a slice of toast.

"Well — maybe you'll turn something up today."

When Jim was gone Paul went out into the crisp early morning air. A few men were on the street on the way to the docks. He walked to the water's edge. Cold wind swept off the Beaufort Sea which had only recently been free of ice at Tuk. He wandered along the shore which was covered with small rocks and various sized pieces of driftwood. He imagined Eskimos in fur parkas paddling kayaks in the icy water. And far out there where the Arctic Ocean still was frozen, maybe the people were hunting seals and polar bears. The sound of the waves washing against the shore was nice. He tossed a rock into the water.

There was no one about. It was as though he was the lone survivor in a deserted village of shacks, cabins and houses in strange Arctic country. Across the bay was the silent DEW Line with its monstrous antennae, masts, radar installations and bulbous

towers, all thrusting their grotesque tentacles toward the clear northern sky.

A high nasal voice interrupted his daydream. "Hey! What you doing there?"

Paul started in surprise. A small man stood beside a log shack near the water's edge. "I guess I was daydreaming."

The man motioned. "You're on private property. Go somewhere else to daydream!"

Perplexed, Paul turned back toward the Lodge. His enjoyment of the morning was gone.

Inside the Lodge the oil heater sputtered and popped as the burner cut out. Paul threw off his jacket and dropped into the big chair. Marie, dust mop in hand, came in. "Back already?" she asked as she dusted beneath the couch.

"Yeah."

"There are books on the shelf. You might like some of Farley Mowat's stories. They're about the Arctic."

"Thanks." He hesitated, then asked, "Who is the man that lives in the log cabin?" He pointed.

Marie laughed. "Abe Gordon. Did you meet him?"

"Yes."

"That shack is his shop in summer. He buys and sells Eskimo crafts, artifacts and relics. Tour groups have lunch here at the Lodge and many of them later buy souvenirs of the Arctic from him. At the end of the summer he ships his merchandise to Vancouver where he has a year-round shop." Marie shook her dustmop outside the door.

"Mr. Gordon told me to get off his property. I was only looking at the water and thinking."

"Abe Gordon is an unfriendly man. He's only interested in making money. He doesn't like people wandering about his property unless they are interested in his merchandise. He doesn't have many friends among the native people for they know how he feels about them. The children give him a bad time." She shook her dustmop again. "Can you find something to do? I have to start soup for lunch — reindeer soup. Think you'll like it?"

"I like caribou steak." He got up. "I'm going to write to my mother and girlfriend and give them my address."

"They must miss you."

"Yeah. Since Mom and Dad divorced, I've spent summers with him. Mom's remarried." He stopped, checking himself from speaking his thoughts about his stepfather.

After a discouraging day of jobhunting Paul returned to the Lodge. In the evening John came. They sat on the porch and talked. "Walter Maniksak, the pilot, said there is a pingo here," Paul said. "Could I see it?"

John tossed his straight black hair away from his eyes. "We'll have to get a key." He glanced quickly at Abe Gordon's shack, then got up. "Maybe my mother needs some caribou meat. Want to go to my place to get the key?"

"Do you live near the pingo?"

"Yes."

"Do you go to the store to get caribou meat?"

"No. I need to go home to get the key to the pingo. That's where the caribou meat is stored."

John saw Paul was puzzled. He hurried to explain. "This pingo is hollowed out on the inside. A few years ago some of our people thought they could chip the ice out from the inside and make a curling rink. I don't know what went wrong, but they changed their mind when it was half done, so our village has a giant refrigerator where we keep things frozen."

"Who owns the pingo?"

"The people."

"That's neat."

John mused. "One person uses more than his share of the space. He has a lot of caribou, wolf and fox hides that take up too much room — and he's not even Inuit." John's tone of voice revealed his resentment.

"What does 'Inuit' mean?"

"It is our word for Eskimo. It means "The People."

As they walked along the dirt street Paul asked, "I've wondered why so many things are out in the yards?"

"What things?"

"Old furniture, boats, gas barrels, snowmobiles — all kinds of things."

John seemed puzzled. "Where else would we put them?"

"I don't know. At home we'd put them in the garage or basement." He stopped. "But you don't have basements because of the permafrost — and I don't see many garages."

"Are your houses big enough to keep everything inside?" John asked in wonder.

"Most everything." Paul glanced at the untidy yards. "And things we don't want we put out by the street and the junk truck picks them up once a week."

John asked, "What do you have in your yards?"

"Nothing. When I was younger my stepfather didn't like me even to leave my bike in the yard.

Typical lawn in Tuktoyaktuk

He said it belonged in the garage."

John looked at the cluttered yards as though he was seeing them for the first time. After a time he said, "I've seen pictures. Do you have short grass and little green bushes and flowers around your house?"

"Yeah. As a kid I had to cut the grass every week." He kicked a soft drink can down the street,

walked on, and kicked it again.   "Carl, my stepfather, made me trim around the flowers and shrubs
with clippers."

Soon John pointed.   "That green house is where I
live."

Two snowmobiles, a canoe with a sleeping dog
inside, three red fifty gallon gas barrels, a big
strip of rusty corrugated metal, a dog sled and some
discarded furniture were scattered to the right of
the house.

"Your home is quite new."

"It's two years old.   Before we built it we lived
with Grandfather and Grandmother over there."   He
motioned toward a log cabin across the street.

John called, "Mother!   Do we need meat from the
pingo?"

Paul followed his friend inside the house toward
the kitchen where a short heavy set woman was stirring something in a kettle on the bottled gas range.
Without looking up she reached for a key on the
window sill.   "Bring a bag of the stew meat and
bones.   We'll have stew tomorrow."   She stepped back
in surprise when she saw Paul.

"Mother, this is Paul Douglas.   His father works
for Dad at the docks."

Mrs. Katoayak held out her hand.   "You're a tall
young man."   Visually she compared Paul's and John's
height.

A girl about thirteen and a younger boy ran in
from the back yard.   Mrs. Katoayak said, "Paul, this

is John's sister, Margaret, and his little brother, Billy."

Billy threw out his chest. "I'm not little! I'm eight years old!"

Paul laughed. "Hi, Margaret and Billy."

Mrs. Katoayak poured boiling water into a teapot. "Would you have mug-up with us?"

Paul was puzzled. Laughingly the woman explained. "'Mug-up' is Inuit for a cup of tea. Our people drink lots of tea."

Margaret placed five mugs on the table before them. They slowly sipped the strong hot liquid.

Billy fumed. "I'll show everyone how big I am when I kill a whale!"

Margaret jeered, "The men won't let you go out in the whale boats."

"Will John go?" Billy asked his mother.

"Of course John will go. He's a man."

John explained, "We're going to whale camp next week. Grandfather and Great-grandfather are taking us because they say Inuit young people are forgetting the old ways."

"Wow!" Paul exclaimed. "You're going whale hunting?"

John nodded. "Dad and Mother used to go, didn't you?"

Mrs. Katoayak's gaze was fixed on the blue waters of the Beaufort Sea. "Whale hunting is a nice time. But your father can't leave his work, and I must stay here to cook for him. I'm glad my children can

Fish drying at Tuktoyaktuk

go hunting the beluga as our people have for hundreds of years. My father and grandfather are right. We Inuit are losing our freedom. We are trading freedom for refrigerators, gas stoves, TVs, radios and Skidoos that the money from regular jobs can buy." She stopped. "But we like those things too."

Putting the key to the pingo into his pocket, John stood up. "I'll get the meat and show Paul the pingo."

"Come again," Mrs. Katoayak said to Paul as the children went out the back door into the sunshine.

A sudden frantic yelping of dogs broke the stillness as five large chained huskies voiced their disapproval of the blond stranger coming from the house.

"Shut up!" John shouted. They quieted immediately.

"Is that your dog team?" Paul asked.

"Our father hunts and traps when he's not working at the docks. He uses the Skidoo most of the time but our grandfather and great-grandfather like the dog team, so we keep them."

The large black and tan dogs eyed Paul suspiciously. "Are they friendly?"

"Not to strangers."

They made their way to the street through the maze of objects at the side of the house.

"That's where we go to school." Billy pointed to a one-story blue building. "I'm in the second grade this fall."

As they walked John asked, "What kind of work do you do?"

"Usually I work in a gas station in the summer. I go to college from September until the middle of May."

John mused. "I'd like that. Maybe next year I'll have enough money ahead so I can go to college."

Children were playing baseball behind the school

building.   "If you come over another day, you can
play baseball with us," Billy suggested.

Most of the players appeared to be of high school
age.   "Maybe tomorrow," Paul said.   "About ten in
the morning?"

"Ten!" Margaret exclaimed.   "We're not up that
early!"

John said, "We stay up late in summer and the
children stay up as late as they want to.   It's nice
being out in the daylight after the long dark winter
days.   Why don't you come over about seven tomorrow
night?   That's when the baseball games start."

Billy dashed ahead.   "Beat you to the pingo!" he
called.

The children ran.   Paul sprinted and passed the
others.   Looking back he saw the children doubled up
with laughter.   John pointed to a grassy hill.
"That's the pingo!   You passed it!"   He spoke
quietly to Margaret and Billy.   "You shouldn't
laugh."

Grinning, Paul came back.   "If it's ice I didn't
think there would be grass growing on the pingo."

John explained.   "Over the years dust and dirt
settle on the pingo.   When summer arrives the frost
leaves near the surface and grass and fireweed grow
in the dirt.   On the inside it stays frozen."   John
took the key from his pocket and opened the padlock
on the wooden door which fitted into the side of the
pingo.

Inside it was pitch dark.   Underfoot there was

Pingo near Tuktoyaktuk

polished ice. "Stand still," John said, "until I find the light."

Margaret giggled. "It's scary. There might be spirits in here. Spirits of caribou and wolves and foxes that didn't want to be killed. They've come back to carry us away, Billy."

As John found the extension cord and bulb which lighted the interior of the pingo the frost glistened in the white light from the single electric bulb. He glanced around. "Where's Billy?" he asked.

Margaret giggled. "The spirits got him."

"Stop it, Margaret!" John went toward the daylight at the door to call his brother.

Paul looked about. It was a weird place. On one side frozen, bloody caribou hides were piled high. Other hides, fox and wolf, were next to the caribou skins. On the opposite side of the pingo were many piles of clear plastic bags containing meat. Some of it was reddish-brown like liver. Paul looked at the sides of the pingo above the meat. The permafrost was beautiful with horizontal glistening streaks of tan, brown, and white. Overhead the white frost hung in hundreds of rounded stalactite-like formations. It was still, so still inside the pingo that Paul could hear Margaret breathing a few feet away.

"I'm cold," she said zipping her jacket about her neck.

John led Billy back to the entrance. "I don't want to go in!" the little boy said, lagging behind.

"There's nothing here but meat and hides."

"And spirits," Margaret giggled.

Reluctantly Billy came inside but he stayed close to John.

Paul picked up a caribou hide. It was frozen stiff. Holding it under the light he admired the brown and white fur. "Does your father hunt caribou?"

"Caribou, wolves and foxes. Hunting and trapping are not as good as they were when Grandfather and Great-grandfather were young. That's why our father works at the docks in summer."

"Would he rather hunt and trap?"

"Most all Inuit would — and the Indians too. But there are more people now, and the oil men are driving the game away. The animals and birds and beluga don't like ships and people."

Paul still inspected the caribou hide. "Are any of these hides your father's?"

"Not now. He sold them to Abe Gordon."

"I don't like Abe Gordon!" Margaret exclaimed.

"Me neither," Billy added. "He's mean!"

"The hides on this side of the pingo belong to him." John motioned to the left. "He buys them from the hunters for a few dollars apiece and takes them to Vancouver where he resells them. He's making himself rich off the Inuit from Tuk."

"Get out of there!" a man's voice snarled. "And you! Put down my hides! How many have you already stolen?"

Paul dropped the caribou hide. John bristled. "We're not stealing your hides. We're after our meat and I was showing my American friend the pingo!"

With upraised fist and anger twisting his face, Gordon made a sudden move toward them. Unexpectedly his leather shoe soles slid, his legs spread wide on the polished ice, and he sat down with a thud. Margaret and Billy snickered. Awkwardly struggling to his feet, his face dark with anger, Gordon shook his fist at them. "Get your meat and get out! And stay out!" he shouted.

LURE OF THE ARCTIC

Margaret and Billy ran outside but John and Paul stood their ground. "Mr. Gordon," John said. "You are using our pingo. It belonged to Tuk before you came. We and the others will come whenever we need some of our meat." Turning his back on the fuming little man he selected a plastic bag of meat and bones and started toward the door. "Let's go, Paul," he said quietly.

"You stay away from my hides, you hear? Or I'll make trouble for you!" Gordon shouted as they went out into the sunshine.

"Wow!" Paul breathed. "He's sure a suspicious man!"

John dropped the plastic bag outside and swung the door shut. As he turned Billy snapped the padlock together. Margaret watched wide-eyed.

John grinned. "You shouldn't have done it, Billy, but he'll soon cool off in there."

They waited a few feet from the pingo entrance. "We'll hear from him soon," John said.

Almost at that instant heavy pounding began on the inside of the door. "Unlock the door! Open up! I'll fix you blasted Eskimos!" Gordon shouted as he rattled the door.

No one spoke. The yelling and pounding grew louder. People came to their doors to watch and listen. An old man shuffled toward the group and Margaret explained what had happened.

"Kabloona," he muttered.

The uproar inside the pingo continued. More

people joined the group, smiling broadly and talking among themselves. At last John said, "I'd better let him out." Quietly he unlocked the padlock and strode back to the waiting group. The door burst open and Gordon staggered out into the bright light.

He glared at the group as he shook his fist at them. "Who locked me in?" he demanded.

"The spirits," Margaret giggled. Everyone laughed.

John stepped forward. "It doesn't matter who locked you in. You have no right to accuse us of stealing your hides."

Gordon pointed at Paul. "He put you up to it. He was trespassing on my property and now he's trying to steal my hides. He's a troublemaker!"

A woman broke in. "We don't take anything of yours. It is you who steal from us because you don't pay our men what the hides are worth."

Gordon turned as he eyed John and Paul fiercely. "Don't you ever lock me in there again!" He stalked off trying to muster his lost dignity.

The group broke up and John locked the pingo. Paul waited staring far out to sea and wondering why Abe Gordon disliked people so much. He must be an unhappy man.

After they left the meat at John's home they crossed the street to visit Mrs. Katoayak's parents in their log cabin home. An old man watched them approach from his seat on the porch.

John said, "Great-grandfather, this is my friend

LURE OF THE ARCTIC

Paul Douglas from the U.S.A."

Paul put his hand out. The little gnome of a man smiled and his deeply tanned wrinkle-filled tooth-less face showed his pleasure as he grasped Paul's hand.

"Great-grandfather is a famous whale hunter," John said with pride.

The old man shook his head. "No. That is for young men. I am seventy-eight — too old for great hunter."

John continued, "But you're going to whale camp next week to teach us young fellows how to catch beluga."

The old man's smile grew wider. "For seventy-eight years I go to whale camp. My mother, Ookanak, and father, Niptanatiak, take me first summer." He dropped Paul's hand. "Kabloona, old Inuit way is good."

"I believe you. I'd like to know more about it."

Margaret ran up the steps to sit beside the old man. "Great-grandfather tells us stories about the old days. Maybe he'll tell us one now."

The aged man nodded. "I cannot remember father," he began. "Mother tell me he go out on ice with dog team to hunt seal. He not come back."

"What happened?" Billy asked, his eyes huge.

Great-grandfather shook his head. "Maybe ice break open and he go in with dog sled. Maybe Nanuk kill him while he watches aglu." He noticed Paul's puzzled expression. "'Nanuk' is Inuit word for great white bear. 'Aglu' is word for hole in sea ice where seals come to breathe."

Paul nodded. "And 'Kabloona'?"

"Kabloona is one not Eskimo. White man."

A woman stood listening at the door. "Grandma!" Billy shouted. "Great-grandfather is telling us stories!"

Margaret added, "True stories about our great-great-grandfather."

The woman smiled. "I heard. Bring friend in. We have tea."

On the kitchen table seven steaming mugs of tea waited. Paul glanced questioningly at the grandmother and gray-haired man who leaned against the refrigerator. John hurried to introduce his grandparents, Mr. and Mrs. Nigiyak to Paul. They shook hands.

Paul said, "It's nice to meet you, Mr. and Mrs. Nigiyak."

"No, no." Mr. Nigiyak objected. "Not Mr. and Mrs. Call us 'Grandfather' and 'Grandmother.' We like that better."

"Mug-up is good," the gnome-like old man commented as he noisily sipped the hot liquid. "Remember Silas, when you are small boy, you go fishing with me? You want stop all the time for mug-up?"

Grandfather's tanned face broke into a smile. "I remember." He explained, "When I was eight, like Billy, we went far to fish. It was near end of winter. There was not food for people. Father knew

kraluarpait, our word for big fish, bite at night."

Great-grandfather nodded. "There was only few families in Tuk then. Long time we catch no fish. People are hungry. I worry how we will eat. One night I cannot sleep. I go to fish. I put line through hole in ice. Fast, big fish take bait. Fish keep biting 'til morning. Then no more."

Grandfather Silas went on. "Father shared fish with rest of Inuit. Next night all men go to fish. I wait 'til they go. Then I go out our log and tent house to follow. That night I fish with men first time."

Great-grandfather smiled at the memory. "You

tell it good, Silas. You remember." He paused a moment. "We catch many fish. Silas ask all time for mug-up. But we eat good raw fish. I taste them now."

Paul's stomach twisted. He choked as he set his mug on the table.

Grandfather laughed. "You not like raw fish?"

"Not much."

Grandmother nodded. "Good. We have now, some-times." She poured another round of tea.

Grandfather reminisced. "Remember Father, how Mother liked kroak?"

There was a far away look on the old man's face. "She was good wife, Atatkloak. She chew hides — sew — cook for me long time. And she cut up and skin whale fast with ulu."

"Ulu is a woman's knife," John whispered to Paul.

"Grandfather, will you take me along with you in the whale boat when you hunt?" Billy asked.

"Wait. Whale hunting is man's work."

Grandmother said, "When we get whale Margaret will help cut up meat."

Margaret beamed. "I'll learn to use an ulu."

"Where will you live?" Paul asked.

"In tent, like old days," Great-grandfather an-swered.

"It sounds great," Paul said to John. "Remember everything so that you can tell me about it when you're back."

"I will."

LURE OF THE ARCTIC

The old man said, "Great-grandson, we show you how to catch beluga so you can teach your children. Must not forget Inuit ways."

After more small talk they got up from the table. "Thank you for the tea," Paul said to Grandmother.

The woman smiled. "Silas and I are Mary Katoayak's father and mother. She is children's mother. Great-grandfather is Esau Nigiyak, my husband's father. He lives with us."

"I see." Paul mentally contrasted Mrs. Nigiyak's loose-fitting pink-flowered summer parka-type garment made in the style of the caribou winter furs of her childhood days with the trim neat outfits worn by his grandmother in Detroit.

Later as Paul and his father ate dinner with the LeBeaus at the Lodge, they talked of Tuk and its people. Peter said, "The Katoayaks and Nigiyaks are fine people. We've known them for three years." He paused, then continued. "As for Abe Gordon, Tuktoyaktuk would be better off without him. We all like money and what we can do with it, but for Gordon, money seems to be his god. The native people in Tuk are friendly if they're given a chance to be. Gordon has made it clear that he is interested only in business."

Paul told of the planned whale hunt. Marie explained, "Only a few families go to whale camp now, and they are mostly the older people. In a few years there likely won't be any whale camps."

The next few days were discouraging ones for Paul

as he continued looking for work. He became acquainted with a few young Eskimo men who were John's friends, and he joined in the baseball games on the school playground.

Two evenings before the Nigiyaks and their grandchildren were leaving for whale camp, Paul, John, the grandparents and Great-grandfather were sitting on the porch. John said, "Great-grandfather, tell Paul about the time when you were small and the polar bear surprised you far out on the ice."

The expression in the old man's eyes changed as he recalled those long ago childhood days. "My mother, Ookanak, hunted and fished like a man to feed us. My father was dead. From time I was big enough, I go with her. When we hunt seal, we take dogs and sled to carry meat home. When sled was empty, I ride, but I walk with mother behind sled when we catch seal." He stopped, gazing at the DEW Line towers with unseeing eyes.

Billy and Margaret came to sit with the others. After a few moments, Billy said, "Tell us about hunting the bear."

Great-grandfather nodded. "Old man like me has many thoughts of long ago time. But you want to know about when Nanuk surprise us."

"Ookanak was hunting seals through ice. She use big hooks to pull up seal when she spear him. We already catch two fat seals. They are beside us on ice. Dogs start to bark. We look. Big polar bear, Nanuk, he comes at us. Dogs jump and bark but they are tied to sled and sled is anchored in ice. They can't help. Nanuk is getting close. He want our seals."

Paul asked, "Did your mother have a gun?"

Great-grandfather shook his head. "No gun. But Ookanak think like man. I look at her. I am scared. Mother pick up four big seal hooks that are tied to sealskin thongs. She swing them in circle around her head and start toward bear."

"Make big noise," she say to me. She squat down swinging hooks faster around head. She go toward bear and make loud noise — like growl noise in throat. She make noise louder until it is like shouts. I squat behind her and growl and yell. Dogs jump and bark.

"Nanuk stop to look at us. Sun shine on big hooks 'til it looks like big circle of light around Mother's head. Bear can smell seals behind us. He snort and start at us again. Ookanak say, 'Yell loud!' Hooks swing around her head. They make zing-g-g sound close to his nose. He quick turn and walk away. After a little way, he stop and look at us over his shoulder.

"Mother jump at him and yell. I jump and yell. The dogs jump and bark. Then Nanuk go away."

Everyone heaved a sigh when the story ended. Margaret said, "Weren't you scared?"

"Yes. Inuit in old times is scared often. Scared of Nanuk, scared to starve, scared of freeze in blizzard. Life was hard then. Inuit must fight to live. Inuit learn young to think fast when danger come in them days."

"Great-grandfather," Paul began, "your stories make me wish I had been an Eskimo in those days when you were young."

The old man nodded. "Kabloona, it sound good now, but was hard. Very hard. In winter we was hungry. People starve. Old people like me can't hunt. They only eat food that hunters need. Old people like me — they go out on tundra to die."

Horror showed on Paul's face. "You mean they went out and froze to death so the others could have food?"

Great-grandfather nodded. Billy's eyes were huge. "Didn't their families stop them?"

Great-grandfather shook his head. "It was only way rest of Inuit can live. We knew it. Old man cannot hunt. Old woman with teeth gone cannot chew hides to make soft clothes. Old people eat food that young people need so our strong Inuit could live through bad times. Long time ago it was Inuit way."

John said, "We aren't hungry now and no one needs to commit suicide so the rest of the group can live. It's better for us now."

Margaret agreed. "And Great-grandfather told me once that when he was small, girl babies were thrown away sometimes."

"Thrown away!" Paul exclaimed.

"Yes, Kabloona. Long time ago, when there was

not food, woman have baby girl and throw it away. No food for baby, maybe better to die fast in cold than starve long time before she die. They throw away baby girl because boy grow up to be hunter to help Inuit live."

Margaret said, "Your mother hunted like a man."

"Yes. But not most Inuit women hunt then. Most chew hides to make them soft. They sew clothes and cook seal, caribou and fish that hunters bring."

Margaret argued. "But you needed women too."

"Yes. Not many throw baby away. Sometimes when mother is near starved she not make milk, then baby have water and little broth. Baby can't live long on water and little broth."

"Did you and Great-grandmother throw any babies away?" Billy asked.

The old man shook his head. "Your grandfather, Silas, only baby of ours that live. A boy and girl die before they are year old."

"Because they didn't have enough food?" Margaret asked.

The old man nodded sadly. In a moment he went on. "That was bad times. We have good times with plenty of game and fish, too. Then we have feasts, celebrations, drum dances and games. In good times we are happy. Inuit know that life is both good and bad."

Everyone was silent, each with his own thoughts. Finally Paul looked at his watch. "I must go back to the Lodge." He got up from the steps. "Thank you, Great-grandfather, for the stories. It will be lonely when all of you are at whale camp."

Great-grandfather looked Paul straight in the eye. "Kabloona, we like you. You want go to whale camp and live like Inuit used to live in summer?"

For a minute Paul was speechless. His eyes went from John's eager face to Margaret's and Billy's smiling ones. "You — you mean go with you for the summer?" he gasped.

"Say yes!" Billy shouted.

"For summer," Great-grandfather repeated.

"Thank you!" Paul said. "I can't think of anything I'd rather do." He hesitated. "But how about Mr. and Mrs. Nigiyak? Is it okay with them?"

John called his grandparents to the door. "We heard you talking. We would like you should go with us," Grandfather said, and Grandmother smiled.

Paul strolled back to the Lodge. Plans for whale camp raced through his mind. This would be a great summer!

THE BOAT TRIP

TO KENDALL ISLAND

Paul pulled the hood of his parka up against the chill Arctic wind. Throwing his bag of clothing over his shoulder he called a goodbye to the Le-Beaus. Sprinting, he caught up with his father who was striding toward the docks.

"You don't mind, Dad, if I go?" he asked.

"I envy you," Jim replied. "It's the chance of a lifetime to learn about the Arctic and the Eskimo customs. And you'll get first-hand information for your sociology course."

As they parted Jim put his arm about Paul's shoulders. "I'll miss you, Son." He strode off toward the docks without looking back.

The sadness which Paul felt at parting with his

father was forgotten in the excitement of loading the decrepit old schooner and barge. Friends and neighbors of the families who were going to whale camp were up early to join in the excitement.

Grandfather and Great-grandfather Nigiyak directed the children as to the items which should be carried aboard. Two other families, Sam and Annie Olorgrak with their grandchildren, Charles and Agnes, and Joe and Rosie Tologanak with their teenage sons, Wallace and Willard, also were going on the old schooner, the **Tuk.**

The noise was deafening as the fifteen adults and children prepared for leaving. Dogs barked as neighbors, friends and relatives stood about offering suggestions and saying goodbyes. Friends of the fortunate children who were going on the whale hunt yelled, wrestled and shoved one another in the excitement of parting.

At last they were off. The ancient Four Atlantic one-cylinder ten horsepower engine put-putted along with its heavy load of humans, dogs, barrels of gasoline and the old barge which would carry home their whale catch. Supplies for the several weeks hunting trip crammed every available space. Grandfather steered the boat which pulled the old barge.

Below deck John, Paul and Charles peered out between cracks in the hull to see where the boat was going. Silently Paul wondered how the decrepit old boat stayed afloat, but no one seemed concerned that water was seeping in in many places. He was glad he had bought heavy boots at the Hudson's Bay Company store.

"Better start bailing," John said grabbing three galvanized pails. They worked silently for several moments. After a time Wallace and Willard took over the task of bailing. No one gave orders but each one in turn did whatever needed to be done.

When they were above deck Paul wondered aloud, "Why didn't Grandfather fix the boat so it didn't leak before we left?"

John shrugged. "It floats."

Charlie agreed. "Yeah, it's okay."

"Someone will have to bail all the way."

"There's plenty of us."

Billy, Margaret and Agnes made their way through dogs, people, cans and supplies. They scrambled on top of a barrel of gasoline. One of the eight dogs on board sat on the next barrel. He nuzzled Margaret's neck. She giggled and pushed him away.

Paul asked, "How far are we going before we start hunting?"

Charles said, "It's about seventy miles to the camp at Kendall Island."

John added, "We will hunt in Kugmallit Bay between the small islands, Grandfather says."

Paul wandered past Grandmother and Mrs. Olorgrak and Mrs. Tologanak. The women were laughing and talking about how good some muktuk and mipku would taste. Great-grandfather and Sam Olorgrak were playing cards. Paul paused to watch.

"Kabloona play cards?" Great-grandfather asked, his eyes sparkling with enjoyment from amid the criss-cross of wrinkles in his bronzed skin.

"A little. But I don't know the game you're playing."

"You learn." The old man turned his attention back to the card game.

Suddenly the put-put of the engine became irregular. Paul glanced at Great-grandfather and Sam. They appeared unconcerned, still engrossed in the card game. He made his way to where Grandfather was steering. The engine sputtered and wheezed for several minutes before it died with one final cough.

Grandfather laughed. "She's done good. Two hours she runs good."

"What's wrong?"

Grandfather shrugged. "We let her drift to shore. We work on her and women get something to eat."

Slowly the waves carried the leaking old schooner with the attached barge toward the stony shore. Great-grandfather and Sam went below deck to take their turn at bailing. Everyone was relaxed and unconcerned, happily accepting the delay. It was as though it was enough that they were on the way to camp and that a balky engine was inevitable.

The brisk northwest wind pushed them toward shore while the men stood about Grandfather as he tinkered. "Could it be a dirty carburetor?" Willard suggested.

LURE OF THE ARCTIC

"Maybe points need fixing," Joe commented.

Grandfather continued dismantling the engine until by the time they were close to shore, parts lay all about him.

The **Tuk** grated against the rocky bottom in shallow water. The three women, their arms loaded with kettles and food for lunch, climbed over the side and waded ashore followed by the splashing children and dogs.

"Go find dry wood," Annie Olorgrak said to Charles and Agnes.

Rosie Tologanak, carrying a kettle, walked a short distance to a fresh water pond. She filled and covered the utensil and placed it on the beach near the dry driftwood which the children had gathered.

Agnes and Margaret ran through the Arctic cotton grass behind the barking dogs. Suddenly honking whistling swans flew in all directions. Immediately the girls were filling their pockets with eggs from the angry birds' nests. Charles and John joined the girls followed by Billy and Paul.

"They're destroying the nests!" Paul complained to John when he caught up to where the dogs were wolfing down eggs as fast as they could break them.

"There's more," John said carefully placing another egg in his parka pocket, "and the dogs have to eat too."

Honking swans, barking dogs, together with the shouting children and chattering women were a com-

Arctic cottongrass

bination of sounds strange to Paul's ears. Momentarily he imagined his mother's reaction to such bedlam should it occur in their suburban neighborhood. When pockets and hands were filled, they returned to the beach.

Grandmother had a hot fire snapping beneath the kettle of water. "It's good the **Tuk** stopped," she said, placing the eggs in a galvanized pail half filled with water. "Swans eggs are good until the middle of July. After that they have little ones in them." She shoved her hood back as she stood near the fire.

The dogs' playful barks changed to fast yips. Rosie dropped the kettle she was holding and ran toward the animals that were struggling with two large honking white swans. Annie and the children rushed to help in the capture. Each woman seized one of the struggling swans, and with a quick twist of the wrist, she wrung its neck.

The women, their hooded mid-calf length parkas flapping in the wind, laughed as they carried the heavy birds back to the campfire.

"Soon they be cooking," Grandmother said seizing her curved ulu and bucket.

"We'll pick the feathers," John volunteered taking a swan from his grandmother's hand.

In five minutes the larger feathers were plucked from the swans. The women held the birds close to the fire to singe away the down and remaining feathers. Then while they kept up a rapid, good-natured chatter, the birds were cut up, tossed into a pail of water, washed and shortly thereafter they were simmering over the fire.

Paul glanced at his watch. Two o'clock. He wondered how long before they would have lunch but he had already learned the Inuit do not live by the clock as the white man does. The men still were huddled about the motor. As the dead engine suddenly sprang to life with its sharp characteristic put-

put-put, they stepped back laughing. Grandfather steered the **Tuk** a short distance westward to a small shallow cove as the children followed along the shore.

Later as the group squatted on the windward side of the fire for a leisurely lunch of boiled eggs, stewed swan, bannock and jam, Great-grandfather asked, "Kabloona, how you like Inuit food?"

"It's good," Paul answered picking a feather from his piece of swan.

"You will like muktuk," Rosie said throwing a bone to a waiting dog. "Just wait."

They lingered over the fire, eating, talking and sipping tea until everyone was stuffed.

"Remember, Silas, when we was kids," Sam said to Grandfather, "and we lived at Shingle Point?"

Great-grandfather and Grandfather nodded. Grandfather lighted his pipe. "We was small but we won't forget that winter."

"Tell us about it," Billy begged as he gnawed the last bit of meat from a wing bone.

Grandfather puffed on his pipe. "Winter was long," he began. "Not much food. Flour and sugar and tea gone." He smiled at Paul. "Inuit must have tea."

Great-grandfather sipped from his mug. "Tea and tobacco."

Sam went on with the story. "Men hunt every day for food, for bear and seal. Whole winter, all we have is frozen fish. Remember, Silas?"

LURE OF THE ARCTIC

"I remember."

Joe mused. "No caribou. It was bad time."

Grandfather continued. "Then Father is lucky. He come from hunting and he have two ugink on sled." He turned to Paul. "Ugink is bearded seal. Very big seal."

He went on. "We feasted. Everyone come to our tent and we eat and eat. Them times it was feast or famine for Inuit. No help from government. Old people and babies die."

Margaret said quietly, "And some old people just went outside and froze to death."

Grandfather nodded. Everyone was silent. After a time Rosie said, "Many things not good now, but better for Inuit than long time ago."

The twins Wallace and Willard who had not joined in the conversation now entered the discussion. Wallace said, "Mother, the old days were better. You didn't have much but the federal government wasn't telling you what to do and claiming your land."

Willard continued. "And you didn't have people polluting our rivers and taking our oil." He paused and then went on. "We were here before the white man. The government says we will be given a block of land with all hunting, fishing and trapping rights. Land that belongs to us alone. It must be a large block of land because it takes ten square miles to support one caribou."

"We might get it — sometime," his father said

drily.

"We should have some say in how the North is developed," Wallace said. "We don't want our land ruined by pipelines. Think what they've done to Alaska. The Inuit were the first settlers in North America. Our people make up forty-five percent of the population of the N.W.T."

"Don't forget the Indians," Sam said. "They are first people too."

"Yeah. Indians make up twenty percent of N.W.T. population, and the rest are newcomers." He glanced at Paul.

Great-grandfather squinted out over the Beaufort Sea. "You think Inuit and Indians should put whites out?"

"No!" Willard exclaimed. "But the native people should have more to say about what happens to our land!"

Grandfather shook his head. "Won't come in my life. Maybe sometime. Changes come slow."

Wallace's usually smiling face was grim. "If it doesn't come soon, then the day of the smiling Eskimo is over."

Sam asked, "You fight government?"

"No. I don't think we should get violent but we should put more pressure on Ottawa so they know how we feel. Maybe then they would speed up the land settlement."

Billy and the girls left the circle and ran over a small rise in the land to the south.

LURE OF THE ARCTIC

"How is it in U.S.A.?" Grandfather asked Paul. "Do Indians and Blacks think like twins?"

Paul nodded. "Long ago our Indians were mistreated and driven from their land, and the Blacks once were slaves in our country. Things are better for them now, but we've had some violence. There's still a long way to go before everyone in our country has equal opportunities."

"Like in Canada," John commented.

Grandmother threw some wood on the fire and added more water to the kettle of fowl and broth. Reaching into a nearby pail she brought out several pieces of dried meat which was tossed into the kettle. The resulting stew would provide them with their next meal.

The sun was warm on their backs. The men smoked as the women packed things away after the meal. Bees buzzed lazily in the sun. Butterflies flitted from one fireweed plant to another. A beetle hurried from beneath a piece of driftwood to another nearby. For some time Paul had been aware of hoarse clacking sounds which reminded him of the muffled quacking of ducks. He visually scanned the shore and water where small frogs hopped about.

"What you look for?" Great-grandfather asked.

Paul grinned. "Something sounds like ducks that have a cold. But I don't see them."

The old man chuckled. "That is wood frogs. Watch — see them jump near the water."

Several two inch long gray-brown frogs with light

stripes down their backs, and with dark eye masks, hopped about the shore croaking loudly.

John said, "Wood frogs do sound a little like ducks. We don't have many amphibians here — only three kinds of frogs and a toad. They have voices. The other reptile we have is the garter snake. He can't make a sound."

Paul nodded, silently staring at the noisy hopping wood frogs. He wondered when they were going back to the boat. No one mentioned moving on though it was already five o'clock. They had traveled only a few miles from Tuktoyaktuk. There were many more miles to go before the whale hunting campsite was reached.

Billy called to the children, "Let's play ring toss!"

"What can we use for rings?" Margaret asked.

"Maybe there are willows over the hill," Agnes said. "We can make rings from them."

When they reached the top of the small rise the younger children waved from the far side of a little lake where a dozen whistling swans and some ducks swam. The children called and motioned for them to come.

As Paul and John descended the ground became wet and marshy. A few scrubby willows grew near the edge of the little lake. They started, then laughed as several swans took off with noisy honks and a flapping of wings.

"Hurry!" Margaret shouted. "There's something

here to see!"

Splashing their way toward the end of the lake their eyes followed the childrens' pointing fingers to a pile of canvas on the ground.

"What is it?" Paul asked.

"Skeletons!" Margaret and Agnes shouted together.

"It's only an old tent," Charles said. "Someone lived here once."

"What's under it?" John asked.

"Skeletons!" the girls shouted again.

Billy ran to stand close to John as his brother said, "Margaret's always talking about spirits and skeletons and now she has Agnes doing it."

"There are skeletons under there!" Margaret insisted. Agnes nodded her agreement.

Billy clung to John's sleeve as he bent to lift the edge of the old tent. As he flung back one side the faded canvas tore apart revealing nothing but bare ground. Billy laughed. "Where are the skeletons, Margaret?"

"Here!" She threw back the opposite side of the canvas.

They stared silently at bare white bones scattered beneath the rotting tent. Billy, wide-eyed, peeped from behind his brother. "Are they people bones?" he whispered.

"Sure they're people bones," Margaret stated. "Animals don't live in tents."

Paul and Charles bent over. "This one is an animal," Paul said.

"It's a dog," Charles replied. "I can tell by the shape of the skull."

"They're all dog bones," Paul said slowly. "But what were dogs doing in a tent with no man?" He pulled away the remaining canvas. A pile of moldy fur gave off a musty odor. He pulled back the top layer.

Horrified they stared at the white skull of a human still wrapped in a musty caribou-skin parka. Billy, panic-stricken, dropped John's sleeve and ran splashing toward camp, closely followed by Margaret and Agnes. Swans honked as the racing children passed near their nests. Over the hill at the camp the dogs barked and rushed toward them.

Deep in the mystery they had stumbled upon, the

young men pulled away the remaining canvas from the fur-encased skeleton.

"I wonder what happened?" Paul said. "Was he sick, or did he freeze to death?"

"Or starve?" Charles added.

"I wonder who he was," John said staring down at the fleshless skull. "Great-grandfather says when he was young many Inuit went out to hunt and never came back. His father, my great-great-grandfather was one of them."

Charles said, "The dogs were in the tent with this man. Maybe he had them inside to help him keep warm."

"Or if he didn't have food, he might have been eating the dogs," John mused.

"Would he eat them raw?" Paul asked.

The young man nodded. "If you're starving you'll eat anything to keep you alive," John said, "even caribou hide, if there's nothing else."

"But there are five dog skeletons here. That would last a man a long time," Paul argued.

"Yeah," Charles said, "but what was he feeding the dogs if he had no food? Maybe the others were kept alive by eating dog flesh, too."

Paul shuddered. "It's gruesome. Imagine dying here alone, freezing to death. Maybe starving for a long time before he died."

The men were silent, staring in disbelief at the gruesome skull encased in the moldy parka. They were roused from their thoughts by the arrival of the remainder of the group. The dogs came first, sniffing and investigating until they were chased away.

As the fifteen people gathered around the old tent and its ghastly contents, Great-grandfather said, "Long time ago he die."

"How long?" Sam asked.

"Long time." Great-grandfather kicked the canvas aside as though he were looking for something. He walked in a circle about the old tent site.

"Remember, Silas, some hunters not come back when we was kids?" Joe said. "Maybe he was one of them."

"Cannot tell," Grandfather replied.

"It is here," Great-grandfather said from a distance of twenty feet. He bent to inspect something in the grass.

Willard asked, "What is it?"

"Dog sled." Bleached almost white by the snow and sun, the sled set where its owner had unhitched the dog team for the last time.

Willard picked it up and looked at the under side. "There's some letters here. Something is carved into the wood. It looks like 'P. G.' with a circle on each side of the letters."

"Peter Grupen," Great-grandfather muttered. "My old friend Peter Grupen."

"You knew this man?" Margaret asked.

The old man nodded. "Long time ago when Silas was baby, Peter went to hunt. He not come back."

"Tell us about him," John said.

They looked down at the remains of Peter Grupen as Great-grandfather began. "We are friends since we are little boys, like brothers." He stopped as his thoughts went back to those long ago days.

"When did he disappear?" Willard asked.

"When we are young men. My wife, Atatkloak and I have Silas. Peter not have wife. One day we go north with dog teams. We hunt bear. Peter have good dog team, better than mine. The dogs go fast across ice. Where they breathe on fur their faces and shoulders are white from frost. Our sleds creak and bump over pressure ice. After long time we stop. We not find Nanuk. We go other ways. Peter go west, I go east. In little while blizzard start all at once, quick. Wind from northwest blow snow so I not see lead dog. The sled creaked on the ice. In few minutes I am in white-out. Sky and snow are like one. I can't see lead dog, I can't see nothing — just snow. I go toward home. I keep wind against right shoulder and find my way by way the snowbanks are on ice. At last I come to Tuktoyaktuk. Blizzard last many days. We wait and listen, but Peter not come home. Maybe he not get wood. Maybe he freeze. Cannot know what happen to him."

Great-grandfather stooped to pull the old tent back over the skeleton. "We leave him. Is what Peter would want."

Silently they made their way back to camp. The men went to the boat and brought back tents. Shortly three muslin tents, one for each family, were set

LURE OF THE ARCTIC

up on the shore.

Because there was a chill in the air they gathered in Grandfather's tent. Some of them sat on the pile of caribou skins at the back. This would serve as the sleeping area. The others sat on the ground near the front of the tent.

Paul glanced at his watch. Nine o'clock. The sun still shone but the temperature was near freezing. He wondered when they would go to bed and where he would place his sleeping bag. Through the open tent flap he could see the fire smoldering beneath the kettles. The dogs lay stretched out, their legs jerking as they chased imaginary prey in their dreams.

Margaret broke the silence. "Great-grandfather, how can you be sure that man was Peter Grupen? Maybe someone else had those initials."

The old man said, "Once in tent, Peter and I was cutting sealskin thongs. When we stop, he make sled. Peter and I not know how to write but we know our initials. Peter cut in wood on crossbeam of sled, like this." With a stick Great-grandfather scratched letters in the soil on the floor of the tent. On each side of the letters, P.G., he made a picture of the sun." (☼ P.G. ☼)

"Father," Grandfather said, "You have found old friend, Peter."

After a time Billy said, "We didn't get willows to make the ring toss."

John grinned. "Go get them."

"I'm not going back to that lake. There's spirits there," Billy stammered.

Margaret and Agnes were silent. They sat close to the women on the pile of caribou hides.

Paul and John went for the willows. When they returned they drove driftwood into the ground for stakes and with the willow twigs they shaped rings. When the equipment was complete the young people played ring toss for a long time.

Billy commented, "Great-grandfather said he and Peter Grupen played ring toss when they were young."

"Inuit have played ring toss for many years," John said. "We have store bought games now, but Grandfather and Grandmother didn't have anything but the games they made."

"It must have been boring in the winter when it was dark all the time with nothing to do," Charles said.

"Yeah," John added. "No school, no books for they couldn't read, and they had hardly any games. But Great-grandfather says that during the dark time they wrestled, told stories and danced. He makes it sound as though they had good times — when they had plenty of food."

John went on. "Great-grandfather never learned to read. There are still many people in Tuk and Aklavik who can't read or speak English. Our Grandmother Katoayak in Aklavik is one of them. I've never seen her, but my father has told me that she is satisfied with the old way of life.

"I like the new ways," Charles said. "When I'm through college I'd like to be a jet pilot and see the world."

"I'll be a teacher. I want to do something to help the Inuit," John said. "I want to write, too, and put Great-grandfather's stories into a book so our people won't forget the old ways, and how it used to be." He was silent a moment before he continued. "But it will be a long time before I'm through college. It takes a lot of money."

Paul said, "I don't know much about the Arctic and the way your people used to live. That's why I'm so excited about going whale hunting. When I'm through the university I'd like to come back here and see all of you again."

"When you come back we three will get together for a reunion," John promised.

"It's a deal." Paul held out his hand and all three shook.

They wandered inside the tent. A lively game of cards was in progress. It was evident from the laughter and wisecracks that Great-grandfather was winning. Paul sat on the ground where he could watch the old man. Silently he wondered at his ability to throw off the sadness he must have felt at finding the remains of his old friend.

When the hand of cards was finished, Great-grandfather said, "Kabloona, you think we not should be happy after we find Peter?"

Puzzled by the old man's ability to know his thoughts, Paul said, "I don't know. I guess I don't understand."

"Old Inuit learn to take bad with good. We not ask why. We kill animals to live. Life for animals or Inuit not long. Peter not live long life like me. No use be sad about Peter — or about me when time comes for me to die."

Paul said, "You're not afraid to die? Those old

LURE OF THE ARCTIC

Eskimo people who used to go out to die in the snow — weren't they afraid?"

The old man stared far out over the Arctic Ocean. "Afraid not right word. Nobody wants to die — but old Inuit know some people's time come early, some late. We have bad times with hunger and sick people, then when good times come, we don't think of bad. Then we are happy. That's why I'm happy now. We go to hunt whales, we have food and good friends are together. We forget bad times."

The women went outside but soon returned with bannock and the kettle of stew. The tent was cold inside, but no one complained. Soon the great quantities of hot stew and tea that were consumed served to warm them.

Finally at one o'clock the Olorgrak and Tologanak families returned to their tents.

"Are young people going to bed early?" Great-grandfather asked. "I think you stay outside for while."

"We'll stay up longer when we get to whale camp," John said. "There'll be more to do when there are many people."

Billy said, "I'm not leaving camp here."

"You're scared of Peter Grupen's spirit," Margaret teased.

"So are you, Margaret," John added.

"I am not!"

"Prove it! Go down to his tent and bring back one of the dog bones."

LURE OF THE ARCTIC

"I don't want to! I'm going to bed." She sorted through a pile of blankets and caribou hides and came up with her sleeping bag.

Grandmother laid the caribou hides on the ground at the back of the tent. John, Billy, Paul and Margaret had sleeping bags but the older Eskimos covered themselves with a blanket and a caribou skin.

With the others breathing deeply in sleep, Paul relived the events of the day. Though it was two o'clock in the morning, outside it looked like early evening. He could hear the waves lapping on the shore. The sound was regular and rhythmic. Swish — swish — swish —

He awoke with a start. John and Grandfather were gone. He got up, quietly rolled his sleeping bag and went outside. Eight o'clock. A heavy fog hung over the sea. The ridge behind the tent was hidden in the mist. His thoughts went to the skeleton beside the lake that had lain there for many years through blizzards, rain, fog and sun.

But where were John and Grandfather? The dogs, too, were gone. There was no sound, only the regular lapping of the waves on the sandy shore. The cold damp air was chilling. He shivered.

For a moment Paul was homesick. He wondered what his mother was doing. It would be lunch time at home. And today was July 4th. The parades were over and everyone was enjoying a holiday. Carl would be at home, fussing about. Their well-watered

LURE OF THE ARCTIC

lawn was the prettiest in the neighborhood with its neatly trimmed shrubs and flowering plants. He had lived there all the years since his mother had remarried — that was the longest time he ever had lived in one place.

And his girl friend, Karen. What was she doing? If he'd been home they would have been together. His father likely was working on the docks. The 4th of July was not a Canadian holiday, and if it had been there would not be time off from dock work in the short Arctic summer.

Dad is a wanderer, he thought. Paul remembered living with his parents in Quebec, Ottawa, Windsor and Vancouver. His father always worked, but he seemed to be searching. His mother said he searched for "the pot of gold at the end of the rainbow." Regretfully, he thought of his father who worked seven days a week. He was not getting to see much of the Arctic.

Down the shore to the left a dog barked. Paul could hear footsteps crunching on the stones. Shortly John's and Grandfather's voices came to him through the wall of fog. He didn't see them until they were a few feet away.

"Hi!" John called. "Grandfather and I have brought our breakfast!" They set two buckets filled with fish on the ground.

"How did you catch all those fish?" Paul asked.

"Put net out yesterday," Grandfather replied.

Within minutes everyone was outside the tents.

Rosie, Annie and Grandmother cleaned fish while Margaret and Agnes helped with other preparations for breakfast.

A driftwood fire soon was snapping on the beach and the fish were cooking. By the time the tea water was hot, the fish were ready to eat. The group gathered in Rosie's and Joe's tent for breakfast. Paul was surprised to find a sheet metal stove had warmed the tent to a comfortable temperature. They threw off their parkas and sat on the ground to eat.

After an hour they went outside. The fog had lifted and the sun was high in the sky. "It's good day," Grandfather said. "We go."

They removed the tent stakes from the ground. Everyone helped with the repacking and loading of supplies. By noon the decrepit old **Tuk** had been bailed out. Supplies, dogs and people were loaded and they were put-putting toward Kendall Island facing into the familiar wind.

Sam steered and shortly Great-grandfather, Grandfather, Joe and Willard were engaged in a game called crazy cards. The game proceeded at a rapid pace with much laughter.

Willard got up. "I'm the loser. Want to take my place, Paul?"

"I don't know how to play this game."

Great-grandfather's wrinkles crinkled even deeper about his eyes. "We show you, Kabloona. Whale hunter must know how to play crazy cards."

The game was easy. After each game the cards were reshuffled, and the loser was replaced by another player. The loser went to take his turn at bailing, and the bailer who was released returned to join the card game. All of the men were included in the fun. Billy and the girls played with the dogs or stood watching behind the card players.

When Sam left the group and relieved Grandfather

who was steering the boat, Paul asked John, "Is your grandfather in charge?"

"There isn't any boss. Everyone pitches in to do whatever has to be done. Everyone takes his turn. Grandfather owns the **Tuk**, but he isn't the boss any more than the others."

"Hm-m-m," Paul mused. "When they included me in the card game, I hope it meant I was included in the work too."

"That's right."

The **Tuk** put-putted along for several hours with no sign of the trouble of the previous day. The sun glistened on the icy blue water.

Soon they pulled into a quiet cove. Within a few minutes they were on shore each one carrying some of the necessary supplies.

Billy and the girls ran through the short grass chasing one another in a game of tag. The dogs, barking, ran beside them. John, Paul and Charles gathered driftwood for a fire. Within a few minutes the water was heating for tea and some of the swans' eggs gathered the day before were boiling in the pail. The women served tea, jam, eggs and bannock which had been brought from home.

By five o'clock everyone was back on the **Tuk** and the card game and bailing were resumed. Paul had decided that the Eskimos liked the old boat to leak. Perhaps it provided them with a necessary activity which relieved the monotony of long hours on the water. But, if the trip was monotonous, no one complained. They traded jobs, laughed and played cards until eleven o'clock, when the **Tuk** was anchored for the night.

On the trip to shore, tents and all night supplies were taken. The dogs picked up a scent as soon as they were on land. With noses to the ground they ran yipping excitedly across the tundra.

Willard rummaged in their pile of supplies, and finding his rifle, he ran after the dogs.

"They're probably on the track of Arctic hare," Wallace explained to Paul as the dogs and his brother disappeared over a grassy rise in the tundra.

Soon the tents were in place and the fire was burning. From across the tundra shots rang out. Five minutes later Willard came over the rise carrying two Arctic hare. Billy ran to meet him. The women already had their ulus and a kettle close by the water in preparation for skinning and cleaning the meat for supper.

"They're big!" Paul exclaimed. "How much do they weigh?"

Willard held the two-foot-long animals by their hind legs as he hefted them. "This one is about eight pounds, and the other about ten." He gave the rabbits to the women who immediately began skinning them.

"They're prettier in winter," Margaret said. "I like them when their fur is white."

"But if they didn't turn brown in summer their enemies could find them," Agnes said.

"An enemy found these even though they were brown," Charles said. Everyone laughed.

Paul continually was amazed at how easily the Eskimos laughed. He wondered if they were always so happy and contented.

Margaret and Agnes saved the hides from the hare. "We will make oopiks," Agnes explained to Paul.

"What are oopiks?"

"Stuffed owls. Abe Gordon gives us a dollar apiece for them."

Margaret exclaimed, "And he sells them to tourists for five dollars!"

"When will we get to Kendall Island?" John asked.

"Tomorrow — maybe next day or day after," Great-grandfather answered. "Are you in hurry?"

"No."

"He's hungry for good whale flipper," Grandmother laughed as she put the kettle of Arctic hare over the fire.

The children shouted and shuddered.

"Why don't you like whale flipper?" Paul asked.

Margaret and Billy held their noses and Agnes gagged. The adults laughed loudly. Great-grandfather chuckled, "You have store food. You not learn to like good Inuit food."

"It's rotten meat!" Margaret exclaimed.

"It smells terrible!" Billy shouted, holding his nose.

"And sometimes it makes people sick. It's rotten meat!" Agnes added.

LURE OF THE ARCTIC

Willard said, "When whale flipper is fresh, it's very good. But after it has aged it smells like Limburger cheese. I don't like it then either."

"It's good," Sam said, "but we don't have it often. We'll have it at whale camp when we get beluga."

"Not me!" Margaret shouted.

After they had eaten, John, Margaret, Charles, Paul and Billy went for a walk on the tundra. They saw Arctic hare, ground squirrels and ptarmigan a short distance from camp. Ducks were swimming in one of the numerous ponds.

John pointed. "There's a fox. He's looking for ducks on their nests."

The fox, his pointed ears twitching, watched them in a puzzled way. "Maybe he's never seen people before," Agnes said. Soon he disappeared.

Finally at 2:30 A.M. they returned to camp. The older people were asleep.

As he crawled into his sleeping bag Paul silently contrasted the Eskimo method of child rearing with that of the white man. Since he had been with the group, not a child had been reprimanded. There was no scolding and no punishment. Yet, none had been called for. The children seemed happy and secure. Before he drifted off to sleep between John and Grandfather, he thought of Tuk and his father, and of his mother and Carl and Karen in Detroit. They were his loved ones and their ways were quite different from those of the carefree Eskimos. Some day he and Karen would be married. He wondered how she would like visiting his friends in Tuk.

The next day they were on board the old boat by noon. Everyone settled into the usual routine of steering, card playing and bailing. The women sat about laughing and talking. Billy and the girls watched as Grandmother showed them how to chew Arctic hare skins to make them soft.

"Young Inuit women not chew skins now," Annie said, "but long time ago a woman was old when her teeth are worn so she cannot chew hides."

Billy said, "Was that when they went out in the cold to die?"

Annie nodded. "Some did."

Grandmother gave a hide to Margaret and one to Agnes. "You chew hides now. Then you make oopiks in camp."

The girls hesitated. "You must know old ways," Grandmother urged. "Boys learn whale hunting. Girls learn woman's work."

Reluctantly they chewed the inside of the hides. "It take long time to make it soft," Rosie said.

Paul, Charles and Billy watched. "Think I'd rather hunt whales than chew hides," Charles grinned. Paul nodded in agreement.

Suddenly the motor began sputtering. A moment later it coughed a final gasp. Sam, who was steering, shrugged and laughed. The men gathered round with much loud talk and joking. No one complained or appeared concerned. It was as though they welcomed the challenge of once again getting the balky engine to run.

Paul watched for a time, then returned to see how the girls were progressing at the hide chewing. Billy stood near the edge of the crowded boat petting one of the black and tan dogs. The northwest wind pushed the drifting boat. They were quite a distance from shore. Paul wondered what they would do if the men couldn't start the motor.

He zipped his parka and pulled the hood over his head. The wind was cold and the sparkling blue water must be near freezing. John had said there likely was ice only a few miles to the north.

A dog growled. Paul turned to see the snarling animal spring from the top of a gas barrel to the back of the dog Billy was petting. The boy stumbled backward as the fighting dogs struck him. He screamed and went headfirst over the side of the boat.

"Billy's overboard!" Paul yelled.

For a moment everyone seemed frozen, fear and horror showing in their faces. Paul rushed to the side. Billy's head bobbed to the surface, then floundering, he disappeared.

Without considering the possible results Paul threw off his parka and kicked off his boots. A second later he was over the side and swimming desperately toward the spot where he had last seen Billy's head. He saw him! After two strong strokes he grasped the boy's hair as he was going down the third time. Frightened, Billy grabbed Paul's neck pushing his head beneath the icy water.

"Let go!" Paul panted when they struggled to the surface. He fought to loosen the crazed boy's hold on his neck. The thought flashed through his mind that soon they'd both drown. Fighting, Billy still hung desperately to Paul's neck, refusing to loosen his choking grip.

Paul felt panic. His heart pounded. Why didn't someone come to help them? They surfaced again. Suddenly Paul drew back his right fist and struck the frantic child full in the face. His body slumped and the choking grip about Paul's neck loosened.

Treading water, he held Billy's face above the surface as he looked toward the boat for help. Grandfather threw a coiled rope. It landed too far away.

"Hold on!" Grandfather yelled, quickly pulling in and recoiling the rope.

They couldn't survive long in the icy water. Paul's arms and legs already were numb with cold. He hoped his fingers could grasp and hold the rope if he reached it. Billy was quiet.

Again the rope sailed toward them. This time he grasped the noose and managed to get it over his head and under one arm. The men pulled them to the side of the boat. Willard, held by his brother, reached down for the stunned little boy and pulled him to the deck.

LURE OF THE ARCTIC

Helping hands were all around Paul as they pulled him onto the boat. He shivered. "How's Billy?" he asked.

Grandfather and the women were gathered around the little boy who had opened his eyes. He struggled to sit up. "Where's Paul?" he whispered.

"Here," Grandfather said. "Both of you are all right."

Dry clothing appeared and they changed in a sheltered sunny spot near the front of the boat.

"Here's blanket," Grandmother said. "Sit where is warm." Her mid-calf parka flapped about her heavy boots.

Great-grandfather stood nearby. His wrinkled toothless face broke into a smile as he held out his hand to Paul. "Kabloona," he said, "you are brave man. We thank you."

Billy said, "Thank you, Paul, for coming for me."

Paul grinned. "I'm sorry I had to hit you."

"Yeah! Why did you hit me?"

"Because you were pushing me under and we'd both have drowned."

"I was scared."

"So was I," Paul replied silently wondering why none of the others had come to Billy's aid.

Grandfather put his hand on Paul's shoulder. "Thank you, my son. Father is right. You are brave man." Sam and Joe nodded.

Wallace and Willard had gone back to tinker with the balky motor. The boat drifted toward the southeast, the direction from which they had come. Charles and John came to sit with blanket-wrapped Paul and Billy.

"You swim good," Charles said.

"Yeah," John agreed. "Some day I hope to learn to swim. Where did you learn?"

"My father taught me. We used to swim in pools and at the beach in summer."

"Our fathers can't teach us," Charles said, "because they don't know how to swim."

"They don't? Why?"

"They never had a place to learn," Charles answered.

John shook his head. "Not many of our people can swim."

"But there's water all around you," Paul argued.

"It's never warm enough to swim in," John explained. "Today is July 5th, and you found out how cold the water is."

Charles said, "You were the only one on the boat who could have rescued Billy because you're the only one who swims."

"Your people have always spent lots of time in kayaks and boats. I'd think you'd be afraid of water if you can't swim."

"We are. Everyone was scared when Billy fell in," John said.

Silently Paul wondered how the group had the courage to set out in the leaking old **Tuk**. Yet they were enjoying the trip, even the bailing and tinker-

ing with the puzzling motor.   He decided their attitude about problems was simply one of acceptance.

Billy threw back the blanket and jumped up.   "I'm
warm now!"   He scrambled to his feet.

As the boy ran toward the back of the boat Paul
wanted to caution him to be careful.   Surely some of
the adults would warn him, but they didn't.   He bit
his tongue and remained silent.

Everyone cheered when the motor started with a
lively put-put.   Paul walked back to where the card
game was in progress.   Great-grandfather got up
slowly.   "Kabloona, take my place," he said.   "I
will bail."

A few hours later after they made camp, the young
men and children searched the land around the nearby
lakes and ponds for swans and ducks nests.   They
returned to camp with a kettle filled with eggs.
The twins hunted in the opposite direction and returned with three ducks and a whistling swan.

"It's cool to live off the land," Paul commented
as he watched the women prepare the meal.   "I'm
beginning to understand how you feel about white
people forcing you to change the way you live."

Grandfather said, "Once much game, many caribou.
Not now."

"There is a reindeer Grazing Preserve south of
here," Willard said, "but we can't hunt there."

"I saw caribou hides in the pingo at Tuktoyaktuk," Paul said.   "Where did they come from?"

"When the weather gets warm in June a few caribou

still come north to Tuk. They come to get away from mosquitoes and flies that are bad farther south. In the old days every hunter took many caribou. Now only a few of our men hunt them. Once big herds came north on Tuk Peninsula for calving in the spring," Willard said, "but not now. There are too many people and machines near Tuk. Now the caribou go farther east where there aren't as many people. Once the Inuit used caribou hides for clothing and we got most of our meat from the caribou. We needed much food for our dogs, too."

The older men nodded. Great-grandfather said, "In old days there was game — Nanuk, seal, birds, fish, caribou, moose. Now caribou and moose not here in winter."

LURE OF THE ARCTIC

"Where are they?" Billy asked.

"South. Winter time they go south to where trees are. When we find ptarmigan, it is good. Ducks and swans gone south in winter too. Only ptarmigan left here. We hunt seals, but is hard and cold. Hunting Nanuk is hard too."

They gathered inside the tent to eat their evening meal. When they were finished Margaret said, "Great-grandfather, tell us about hunting seal in the old days." She started chewing the Arctic hare hide which was slowly softening.

Great-grandfather settled back with a happy smile on his wrinkled face. "It is good to tell young Inuit about how it was here. When old ones are gone, you tell children."

"I will put your stories in a book," John promised, "so all Inuit can remember how it was."

"Is good. You tell them better. You have education." He turned to Paul. "Kabloona, I not learn English until Silas is little boy. I not know how to read." He spoke sadly.

"But you were always working to feed your family. You were a great hunter," Paul said.

"No, Kabloona. Many times I have no food for my family."

"Tell us about hunting seal," Margaret said again.

"Peter Grupen and I hunt together," Great-grandfather said.

Wide-eyed, Billy asked, "Peter Grupen the skele-

ton?"

"Yes. We are good friends. Like Silas and Joe and Sam, me and Peter grow up together. We go on ice with dogs and look for seals' breathing holes. Dogs sniff in snow until they find hole. Then we run harpoon down in snow 'til it go in water."

"That was where the seal came up to breathe?" Billy asked.

"Yes. Every seal have ten, fifteen holes where he go to breathe. We try to find more than one. Then we stand over hole with harpoon. Have to be quiet or seal use another hole if he see something move. We keep dogs away or seal hear noise and go away.

"Was cold. Sometimes fifty degrees below zero. We put our feet in caribou fur bags and warm one hand at time in sleeve of other arm. We wait. Sometimes seal don't come for many hours. But we must be ready.

"When one come, quick we push harpoon down. If we miss, seal go away and not come back. Harpoon was fasten to thong with stick tied to it. Was so seal not get away while we chop ice around breathing hole big enough to pull seal out.

"Seal's very heavy. When they fight it is very hard to get one out of hole and on ice. We are happy when we get seal. We have good food again. We eat a lot when we get seal, maybe ten pounds of meat a day. We share seal with families that not have food. We eat together and have good time."

"How could anyone eat ten pounds of meat in a day?" Margaret asked.

Great-grandfather smiled. "Was good, the seal blood soup and blubber and seal meat."

Agnes and Margaret wrinkled their noses. "Ask Grandmother if it was good," the old man said.

The women nodded. "Was good," they said.

Sam took up the story. "When I was small, Inuit believe seal has soul that will be born again in another seal. That way, same seal could be caught many times."

"Do you believe that, Great-grandfather?" Charles asked.

"Who knows? Have seen shaman do things we do not understand. Maybe seal soul live many time in other seals."

Charles asked, "What have you seen a shaman do?"

The old man explained to Paul, "Kabloona, shaman is Inuit man that can do things other men not know to do." He paused, his eyes gazing toward the sea as he remembered the distant past.

"Once Palvik, my uncle, was sick. He have bad pain in belly. Can not eat or sleep. Was cold in winter, but Palvik was hot. He hold side and roll on sleeping place. Shaman Utuggouq come and open Palvik to take out evil spirit that make him sick. Palvik gets better fast."

Paul asked, "Did he operate on Palvik?"

Great-grandfather shook his head. "He take out evil spirit but he not cut Palvik open."

"Why didn't the man have a doctor?" Billy asked.

"Shaman was doctor. He cure sickness. Sometimes he tell us where caribou and fish are."

Paul glanced at Willard who winked knowingly. A half-smile played about the corners of John's mouth. Though the young Eskimos did not believe the shaman could perform miracles they did not dispute the old man's beliefs.

"Why did the people starve if the shaman knew where the fish and animals were?" Billy asked.

Great-grandfather shook his head. "Shaman can do things most men not know how. They hunt and fish and have wife and family like other Inuit men.

Shaman can do other things, too. But some things they cannot do. Like doctor now, sometimes cannot keep sick person from die."

No one spoke. In a minute Great-grandfather went on. "Young Inuit now not believe shaman can drive out evil spirit — that he have great power."

"We have priests, ministers and missionaries," Margaret said. "We go to church and pray to God."

The old man said, "I remember when a minister, Mr. Whitman, poured water on our heads. I was young boy. We did not know why he did it."

"Why did he do it?" Billy asked.

Margaret said, "He baptised them."

Great-grandfather nodded. "Inuit has changed. Some things not good for Inuit. We change and soon we not be Inuit if we do things like white man all time. Our young men drink liquor. Whiskey is bad for young Inuit. Make them do bad things."

Paul inquired, "Don't any of this group drink?"

Great-grandfather shook his head. "We don't ask ones who like whiskey to go whale hunting."

Grandfather Nigiyak commented, "Whale hunting is dangerous work. Need men to think quick on whale hunt. Some things are good now. We not want to give up some of white man's ways. I not want to live in tent in winter again." He smiled.

Great-grandfather agreed. "When I was young man, I am happy. I like tent. Was not cold for me then. In winter we pile dirt around outside and put tent on top. Now I am old man, I like warm house in

LURE OF THE ARCTIC

winter. But we must remember old ways. That is why it is good to go to whale camp. Young people," he motioned toward the children and young men, "must know how it was then. Something bad will happen if Inuit do not stay together and remember old ways of our people. We cannot be like white man in all ways."

4

WHALE CAMP

Gray damp Arctic air penetrated jackets and parkas as the **Tuk** with her cargo of humans, dogs and
supplies plowed through the waves. Small islands
began to appear and the **Tuk** made her way between
them. "Might be beluga any time," Sam said.
"Whales come where Mackenzie River goes into Beaufort Sea. They have calves in summer in water
between little islands and Kendall Island. Maybe we
find them soon."

Anticipation was high as they neared the end of
the boat trip. The card game had ended. Everyone
wanted to be the one who saw the first whale.

Willard was relieved from bailing by Charles. He
came to stand near his father who was speaking.

"Soon no more whale camps. Every year more Inuit get jobs, like your father, John. Older Inuit come hunting few years, then no more."

Agnes took her father's hand. "We will tell the children at home how it is at whale camp, Grandfather."

Sam nodded. "You remember to tell friends and when you grow up, tell your children."

"Why aren't there as many whales as there used to be?" Billy asked.

Willard answered, "Because the water in the Delta is polluted. Oil and chemicals are carried here from up the river." John and Charles nodded their agreement.

"There's one!" Billy shouted pointing to a white whale about the size of a dolphin. A puff of condensed moisture rose in the air as the whale surfaced to blow.

"That's a whale?" Paul said questioningly.

"Beluga are whales but they're smaller than the other kinds," John answered.

They watched the graceful pure white creature glide through the water toward them, then suddenly veer to the right into deeper water.

"She hear motor," Grandfather said.

"It is good sign," Great-grandfather murmured. "Good sign to see whale on way to camp. Will be good hunt."

Slowly the **Tuk** put-putted along between small islands near the south shore of Kendall Island. "I see tents!" Billy pointed to the northwest.

"There is camp," Grandfather said.

Great-grandfather shielded his eyes and squinted toward shore. "My eyes not see tents."

Margaret said softly, "There are six tents, Great-grandfather."

"And we will have three, so there will be nine tents at whale camp," Billy said proudly demonstrating his knowledge of numbers.

When the little schooner pulled into the shallow cove near the camp, women and children gathered on the shore to welcome the newcomers.

"Where are the men?" Agnes asked her grandmother.

"Whale hunting. See? Schooners are gone. Only barges here," Annie replied.

They landed amid much shouting and laughing. Like their group, most of the people appeared to be middle-aged or older. When they were on shore a gray-haired stout woman rushed to greet Grandfather and Grandmother.

"Silas! Susie!" the woman shouted. Suddenly she stopped to look closely at the young people who were unloading supplies from the **Tuk**. She pulled on Grandfather's sleeve, talking in Inutitut. She pointed to John.

Grandfather smiled. "Your grandson, too," he said softly.

He shouted, "John! Margaret! Billy! Come!"

"What is it?" John asked looking from Grandfather to the woman who stood waiting.

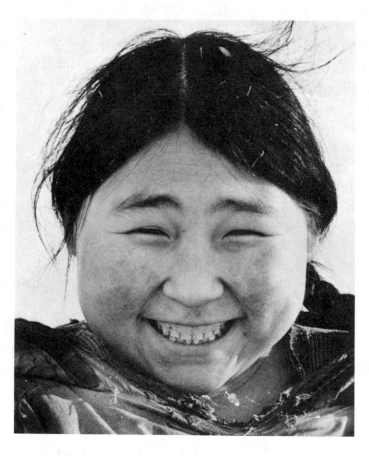

Grandfather said, "This is your Grandmother Ka-toayak."

Suddenly there was great confusion with everyone talking, shouting and laughing at the same time. Much of the conversation was in Inutitut.

Paul, standing at one side by himself, was puzzled by the strange scene. He understood that this woman was Mrs. Katoayak and that she was John's,

LURE OF THE ARCTIC

Margaret's and Billy's grandmother, but he understood little else that was happening. After half an hour of Eskimo language conversation, the confusion lessened and the women set about making tea. While they sat on the ground for their mug-up, Grandfather introduced members of the new group to the young people and children. Paul heard a woman murmur, "Kabloona" as she looked at him. He smiled at her and nodded.

When there was a lull in the conversation Paul said to the woman, "Great-grandfather calls me 'Kabloona' too."

She shook her head to indicate she didn't understand. Grandfather said something to her in Inutitut.

"Whale hunting is good?" Grandfather asked a woman named Nellie.

"Not many whales," she replied. "Not like long ago. We caught one, but most time — nothing." She motioned toward the tents. "Good to be here." She gazed out over the waving grass of Kendall Island.

"We saw a whale," Billy announced.

"One — yes. Years ago — many, many," Great-grandfather murmured.

Abruptly Willard jumped up tossing his metal cup on the ground. He strode back and forth before the seated Eskimos. In an angry tone he said, "For years we've talked about how bad hunting is! The whales are almost gone, the caribou and foxes are going, the fish are being poisoned! They're drilling offshore wells in the Beaufort Sea! Do you know what that means? Oil spills and polluted water! Soon the ducks and swans will go and the polar bears will leave! Seals and fish will die! And on land they talk about building a pipe line that will pass through the best hunting land near Aklavik!"

Joe nodded. "Inuit need land and sea to live in old way."

Sam spoke to John and Charles. "You young men have education. Can speak and write English good. You and Willard and Wallace know Inuit problems. All of you must speak for the Inuit to save Inuit way of living. If the government signs the final agreement of land claims, things will be better. You must see they don't forget."

"We will try," John said quietly. Charles nodded.

From the distance the sound of boat motors drifted over the water. Someone shouted, "The men are coming!" The children jumped up.

As the two schooners docked the middle-aged and elderly men hurried to greet the newcomers, and again the confusion of the earlier scene was repeated as Grandmother Katoayak took her grandchildren to meet their grandfather.

"We have fine Inuit grandchildren, Silas," Grandfather Katoayak said limping to stand beside Grandfather Nigiyak.

"We do, Ishmael," Grandfather replied.

At the five o'clock evening meal Paul and the

LURE OF THE ARCTIC

Katoayak and Nigiyak families ate together in the Katoayak tent. Ella Katoayak had prepared a large pan of baked whitefish and Susie Nigiyak furnished bannock, jam and tea. After the meal they talked for a long time. Paul was amazed at the ease with which John, Billy and Margaret conversed in Inutitut, and though he understood little that was said, he observed closely.

After a time his mind wandered. He tried to imagine Ella Katoayak in the company of his mother and grandmother in Detroit. Her stringy gray hair, deeply lined dark face with the twinkling eyes, her pudgy parka clad body and lack of knowledge of the English language would instantly set her apart from his relatives and their friends. Mrs. Katoayak would be unhappy in the group and his mother and grandmother would be uncomfortable with her. And Grandfather Katoayak — Paul wondered why he limped. What had happened to cause him to be handicapped?

He thought of Wallace and Willard. All at once he understood the fervor with which they argued for the continuation of the former Inuit way of life. Previously he had thought they were rather radical. But now he understood that the old Inuit way of life was their heritage. He hoped the white man would not force his ways upon them.

For two days the wind was too strong to permit whaling so the men remained in camp. Smoking and card playing, with lots of laughter, proceeded at a rapid pace. The white muslin tents were kept comfortably warm by burning driftwood in sheet metal stoves. Fuel was no problem since the beach of the island was covered with windrows of wood which had been carried downstream by the Mackenzie River.

Paul, John and Charles also played cards but part of the time was spent roaming over the tundra of Kendall Island. Billy and three other young boys from whale camp wandered about hunting with sticks, stones, sling shots and crude bows and arrows. They were successful in killing several ground squirrels and a whistling swan. The girls gathered bird eggs. Food was plentiful.

By the second day Paul was restless. "Will the men go whaling today?" he asked.

"If the wind doesn't blow too hard," John said. He tossed a stick into the water. It bobbed on the waves, then washed back on shore. "Wind's too strong for whaling," he said. "Let us walk along the shore." They pulled their hoods up against the gusty northwest wind and started toward the west.

"What's this?" Paul asked motioning to the remains of a log house.

"It looks as though it was a log building once. Maybe someone lived here," Charles said kicking aside a rotting log. "Here's an old whaling harpoon!" he shouted.

"I've found a rusty trap!" Paul shook the soil from the old piece of metal.

A roughly made chair with two broken legs and a rusty little kettle completed their discoveries.

LURE OF THE ARCTIC

The wind had increased in intensity as they poked through the ruins of the old building. They started toward camp. The wind pushed hard against their backs.

"It's never this cold in Detroit in summer!" Paul shouted.

Charles yelled, "In the Arctic it can be hot or cold!"

Inside the tent the Katoayaks and Nigiyaks sat about the metal stove drinking tea. The slightly raised rear half of the tent was piled high with furs and quilts. Here the women and children relaxed as Grandmother Nigiyak taught the girls how to sew their oopiks made from Arctic hare fur. The men and boys sat on the ground at the front portion of the tent.

"Br-r-r, it's cold outside," Paul commented tossing his parka to the side of the flapping tent. He helped himself to the tea and squatted beside Great-grandfather. "It's cold enough to snow — but it doesn't snow in July."

"Sometimes," Great-grandfather replied. "Once when old Dennis was here, wind blow three days. Snow come, like winter. We not go out in boats, but wait in tents."

"Who is old Dennis?" John asked.

Great-grandfather sipped his tea before he answered. "Was one of our people. Many years he live on island. Had four log buildings. One was good house."

"Hey!" John said. "We found the place where the buildings were. Did he live alone?"

"With family," Great-grandfather said. "About 1930 he was rich Inuit."

"Not many rich Inuit," Grandfather said drily. "Old Dennis had record player and typewriter. For long time house was there when other buildings are gone. Inside was record player, rifle, traps and whaling harpoons."

"Could he type?" Margaret asked.

Grandfather shook his head. "Old Dennis not read or write. He make money selling furs. He wants things because they are new machines for him. After he died nobody lived in the house. Furniture and record player and typewriter was in house 'til it fall down."

Paul asked, "Why didn't someone use the things that were good?"

Everyone looked at Great-grandfather. Finally the old man said, "Old Dennis' spirit live there."

Margaret giggled. "The house was haunted. There are ghosts around here, Billy. You'd better not go near old Dennis' place."

John smiled but the older Eskimos did not laugh when Billy hurried to sit close to Grandfather Nigiyak.

Paul opened the tent flap. "It's snowing!" he shouted.

The children threw on their parkas and rushed out into the wind and snow. "It's a blizzard!" Billy yelled. His shouts brought Margaret, Agnes and Charles. Soon a snowball fight was in progress. Anyone who appeared was a target until the next victim came out. Before it was over nearly every person in camp had joined in the fun.

Back in the tent again card playing was resumed. Margaret placed a loop of string over her thumb and little finger. Hesitatingly she said to Grandmother Nigiyak, "Show me how to make a string caribou."

Her grandmother shot a glance at Great-grandfather. "Not good to play string games in summer," she said softly.

Margaret giggled. "You think evil spirits might come?"

The two grandmothers exchanged glances. "Great-grandfather dropped out of the card game. "You make string figures, Margaret?" he asked.

She shook her head. "I don't know how. I want to make the caribou running if Grandmother will help me."

The old man shook his head. "Should not play string games in summer — only when sun is dark in winter. Bad things come if we play string games in summer. Bad weather, no whales or somebody get sick."

John smiled. "Maybe old Dennis' spirit sent the snow storm because Margaret has been making string figures. That will teach you, Margaret."

"Be quiet, John," she said as she turned to Great-grandfather. "There isn't any sun today, the tent flap is closed so hardly any light gets in, and it's snowing. If old Dennis' spirit is out there, he'll think it is winter."

For a time Margaret silently experimented with the string. "Please help me, Grandmother," she begged. "None of us young Inuits know how to make string figures."

Great-grandfather nodded. "Show her. Afterward I will drive evil spirit away. Young Inuits need to know Eskimo string games. Over many years Eskimo families have good time making birds, people, animals from string. Story goes with each string figure. Susie, make fox and whale."

Grandmother Nigiyak placed the long loop of string over her thumb and fingers as she chanted, her voice rising and falling. Then, too fast for the eye to follow, she arranged the string into three loops on each hand. Fingers flying as she chanted in Inutitut to the movements — dropping and interchanging loops, drawing one over another, changing them from one finger or thumb to another. When she raised her hands to show the finished figure everyone could see the fox and whale. The children laughed.

Billy sighed. "That old whale was stranded on shore and the fox was having a good dinner when the Eskimo chased him away."

Paul asked Mrs. Nigiyak, "Were you telling the story as you chanted and made the string figures?"

Susie nodded, her broad face crinkling into a

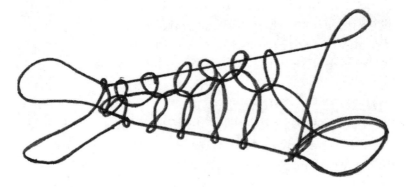

String figure people dancing

smile.

Grandfather Katoayak said, "When Silas, Susie, Ella and I was young we learn to make string figures and the story that goes with them." He spoke to his wife. She nodded and took the string from Susie.

With flying fingers she formed two men facing each other. As she chanted she indicated which man was talking by holding one hand out, and the other in, alternating, she changed their positions as she chanted. John translated for Paul.

* "I'm going to shoot that bird, I made it fly."
The other hand came out.

"I'm going to hit it with a stone, too, even if
you did make it fly."

"Your grandfather has no knife."

"Your grandfather has a knife made of whalebone."

"Your grandfather has no boat."

"Your grandfather's boat is made of rotten boot
soles."

"Well, let's fight it out."

Ella rapidly pulled the loops through one another
to show the men fighting and finally the string
figure was broken up.

Paul said, "At home we children used to make
cat's cradles from string, but there wasn't a story
that went with it."

For a long time the string games continued as
Margaret's two grandmothers taught her. Finally
Great-grandfather said, "We stop now and I will
drive out evil spirits."

The old man took the string from Margaret and
quickly formed a figure as he sang a threatening
chant which ended with, "Be off with you!" He
shuffled toward the tent flap, manipulating the
string figure until at last it broke up. He returned to where Margaret sat. "Do not make string
figures again 'til winter. You not know how to
drive away evil spirits," he warned.

---

*Vera Fidler, "String Figures," **The Beaver,** Winter, 1963.

Margaret smiled. "Yes, Great-grandfather."

John pulled back the tent flap. "The storm is over," he called. The water beside Kendall Island sparkled clear, cold and blue.

"A fox!" Billy shouted pointing toward a rise in the land. The dogs rushed barking toward the gray animal which disappeared over the other side of the bluff.

Margaret giggled. "That's old Dennis coming to get us." Billy ran to stand close to John.

"She's teasing," the young man said softly.

Next morning only a few traces of the snow remained and the water was calm. Willard and Sam had gone to the bluff behind the camp to search the water for whales. Soon Willard came on a run to announce, "They're blowing! Let's go!"

A few minutes later three schooners, the **Tuk**, the **Inuvik** and the **Aklavik** left camp to pursue the whales. John, Charles and Paul were included in the crew of the **Tuk** with Grandfather Nigiyak, Great-grandfather, Sam, Joe, Willard and Wallace.

"It seems strange without the women and girls," Paul remarked to Sam.

"Women's work not whale hunting," he replied. "Too exciting and dangerous. Women will work at camp if we get beluga." Sam rubbed the stock of his rifle until it glistened. Charles went to replace Wallace at the task of bailing. Grandfather steered the **Tuk** and the rest of the crew stared over the water searching for white whales. Excitement was high.

"There's one!" Willard shouted as a puff of condensed moisture rose ahead of them.

The little schooner sped toward the spot where they had seen the whale blow. Every man except Grandfather and Paul held either a harpoon or a rifle.

Paul studied the harpoon held by Joe. It was a heavy wooden pole with a detachable bronze point at the end. The point was fastened to a strong line about forty feet long, while the other end of the line was attached to a sealed empty oil drum with about half the line wound about it. The rest of the line was coiled on deck.

Though he disliked leaving the excitement of the moment, Paul went below to relieve Charles at bailing. Through the cracks in the hull, he peered ahead. One of the other schooners was slightly to the right of the **Tuk**. He wondered what was happening on deck. Had they sighted the whale again? The monotonous task of bailing continued until John came to take over.

"We lost her," John announced.

Back on deck preparations were made to beach the boats on a nearby island to await the arrival of other whales.

On shore Paul and John searched for eider ducks' nests. As they roamed over the small rock-covered island plump lemmings scurried through patches of Arctic cotton grass. Joe and Great-grandfather set out a gill net for herring.

"The dogs would have a feast here," Charles observed as he slapped a mosquito on his wrist.

"I've wondered," Paul began, "why you don't feed your dogs?"

"They hunt for their food in summer," John explained. "They find lemmings, birds and eggs, mice, Arctic hare, fish — there's plenty of food for them in summer. We feed them in the winter."

"It must take a lot of dog food."

The men laughed. John said, "We don't feed them dog food. We give them frozen fish, caribou, seal — any kind of animal meat we can get."

Paul paused to watch a fat Arctic bumble bee secure a load of nectar from a purplish-rose stalk of fireweed. Soon he flew away, buzzing, his hairy body yellow with pollen.

"There's a ptarmigan." John pointed to a reddish brown and black bird about fifteen inches in length.

It was some time before Paul could see the bird because the color blended so well into the background of lichen-covered rocks and scanty brown vegetation.

He commented, "Grandfather said he used to hunt ptarmigan in winter, so they don't go south like the swans and ducks."

"They are here all year," John answered. "Hardly any birds can live through an Arctic winter. Ptarmigans' feathers turn white in winter so they're hard to see against the snow. Their feet are cov-

ered with feathers then, too. Snowy owls, the oopiks, are white in winter also."

"Why are ptarmigans' feet covered with feathers
only in winter?" Paul asked.

John answered, "The feathers protect their feet
from cold and they spread out on the snow. They're
like snowshoes and this prevents the birds from
sinking in soft snow."

"Hm-m-m." In a moment he asked, "What can they
find to eat in winter?"

"Willow buds and small twigs. They can stand the
cold but when a frost follows a thaw so their food
plants are covered by ice, many of them die."

Charles said, "Ptarmigan have an interesting way
of getting into their sleeping spot. Instead of

walking, they plunge into the snow flying and when they leave their burrows they fly up instead of walking away. So, no tracks lead to their sleeping spot."

"That's pretty smart," Paul said.

Charles continued, "Arctic hare and foxes and weasels also turn white in winter."

Paul stared at the ptarmigan. "He looks like our grouse," he observed. "Do you eat them in summer too?"

"You bet!   They're good any time," John answered. "Great-grandfather tells of winters when the people couldn't find game and they were starving. If they found a flock of ptarmigan, their lives were saved."

All this time the bird sat very still believing that he had not been discovered. Paul cautiously bent over to study him. Everyone jumped when the ptarmigan suddenly shot up to a height of thirty feet before starting a downward glide as he cackled a call that sounded like, "Grrr, quack, quack, quack, go back, go back!"

They laughed. Charles said, "It's easy to kill them by throwing rocks because they sit still so long. But we have plenty of food. There's no need to kill birds or animals unless there is a reason."

John pointed. "There's a sik-sik. There's a colony on that ridge."

"He looks like a prairie dog," Paul said.

"They are Arctic ground squirrels. Sik-sik is the Eskimo name for them," Charles said.

John said quietly, "Watch. In a minute he'll warn the others."

Sitting upright on his haunches the little animal eyed the intruders suspiciously. Then the warning cry, a short chirping bark, "Sik-sik-sik-sik!" rang out. Round furry heads popped up between the gently waving cotton grass until the entire colony of animals was sitting bolt upright. When they spied the young men they began the warning cry which was picked up by the little neighbors who now had risen on their hind legs as they tried to locate the enemy. When the men slowly approached the colony the barks changed to loud screams, and finally the animals disappeared into their tunnels in the sandy ground.

"Sik-siks make nice pets," Charles said. "I had one when I was small. He ate anything we did. He liked cereal, raisins, caribou meat — just about anything I gave him. They're not as big in summer, but before they hibernate in October they weigh about three pounds."

"Sik-sik are good food for us," John added. "We had some the other day. Billy and the other little boys got two or three with their sling shots. We also hunt them for their skins. We call them parka squirrels."

Charles went on. "They have lots of enemies, men, foxes, bear, wolves, dogs and snowy owls. Lots of sik-sik are caught, but there's always more. A female has five to eight in a litter and they have more than one litter in a summer."

Back at the shore the men were drinking tea and eating bannock which had been brought from camp. When they finished lunch, they smoked, their eyes constantly searching the water for whales. Bees buzzed everywhere and yellow, black and white butterflies flitted from one fireweed plant to another.

Fed and relaxed in the warm sunlight, Paul daydreamed. His father would be working at the dock. Again he felt a pang of regret that his father was not with him to enjoy the experiences of the trip. They were similar in their likes. And his mother and Carl — what might they be doing? The usual routine he expected. Work, shopping, visiting relatives and fussing about the house. Somehow, with many miles between them, Carl didn't seem as fussy. And Karen? Did she miss him?

Paul roused himself as John was saying, "Great-grandfather, tell us about the old days when you were a great hunter."

The old man squinted into the sunlight. The wrinkles and creases in his weather-beaten face shifted, and his dark eyes sparkled with pleasure at John's request. His white hair ruffled in the gentle breeze.

"Was time for spring," he began, "but spring not come. People are hungry. Was storm. Wind blow snow so we cannot see far from sod and driftwood house. In house I fix dog team's harness, tell stories, sleep and wait. Was hard. We are hungry."

The old man looked at Paul. "Kabloona, Inuit learn long time ago that in Arctic we take whatever happens. Sometime, bad time ends." He paused, remembering the old days.

Everyone waited patiently for Great-grandfather to go on. After a time he continued. "Dogs are hungry. I have only a little frozen fish for them. I go outside. Wind and snow hit me hard. Could not see dogs. I know they are close to house where there are drifts. I poke in drifts in humps in snow 'til a dog whines. I find chain and pull him out of bed under snow. I pull him out or he will get so deep in snow he cannot breathe. When I pull all dogs out I give every one a small fish. That is food for day. Not enough. Dogs are hungry.

"When dogs are under snow drifts, sometimes their heat makes snow melt and it freeze. Make ice coat over them. Dog cannot breathe and he die. That is why we pull dog out of snow where he is warm.

"After a few days, storm stop. My friend, Nasarlulik, go with me. We go for seals. Nasarlulik had sleds and dogs for two teams. He have fourteen-year-old boy, Kiogiak. Kiogiak drive one team. We start with harpoons, dog teams and sleds. We know place where there are many seal breathing holes. It is hard to get over high pressure ridges."

Paul interrupted. "What are pressure ridges, Great-grandfather?"

Several of the men got another mug of tea as the old man explained. "Kabloona, by spring ice is five feet thick, but is not smooth. Wind and tide break ice many times. Water moves ice and it piles up and freezes and long ridges are there. Sometimes many ridges. It is hard to get dog team over pressure ridge when they are pulling sled."

Paul nodded and Great-grandfather went on. "After while dogs find open breathing hole. Kiogiak want stay by himself to hunt seal. He was strong boy, almost a man. His father leave him and we go over more pressure ridges. Dogs find breathing holes for us. Nasarlulik was far out on ice, I was in middle and Kiogiak was close to shore. We not see each other because ridges of ice are too high. We not hear because wind blow hard.

"We get harpoon ready. Very quiet. Seal are smart. They hear sound or see something move, they go to different breathing hole for air. My harpoon was ready. I bend over hole. Is cold, but must be still. I remember we need meat.

"Seal has ten, maybe fifteen breathing holes. He comes up to breathe at hole about once in five minutes. He feed under ice 'til he have to get air."

Paul asked, "Why don't the breathing holes freeze over?"

"Seal is smart." The older men nodded. "When ice is thin in fall, seal breaks hole. He makes many holes. He know how to keep them open. He break thin ice by scratching it with flippers. Ice around hole gets thicker, but he not let hole freeze over hard."

Grandfather Nigiyak puffed on his pipe, his eyes constantly searching the nearby water for a spouting whale.

The old man, lost in memories of the past, went on. "I sat on snow block and put feet in caribou hide fur bag to keep warm. I put swansdown lure over breathing hole so it will move when seal comes to breathe. Harpoon is ready. Steel head on harpoon is sharp. It is fastened to harpoon shaft and to leather thong about forty feet long. Steel shaft is made so it will come off when it goes through seal's hide. I sit still for long time. I wonder if Kiogiak is tired. Is exciting to be fourteen-year-old and hunt alone for first time. I think of hungry people. We will have big feast if we get seal. Women will make seal blood soup and we have good seal blubber and meat. We will laugh and eat and eat. We forget hungry feeling and eat 'til we cannot eat more.

"Then, there was seal! I grab harpoon. When he come up I push it down hard with all my strength. I feel all way up my arm when harpoon smash into seal's head. I hurry to chop ice to make hole bigger. With harpoon in him the seal pulled and wiggled to get away. I wrap end of line around left foot and try to pull seal up. It try to get away. Then I get him out on ice and kill him with shaft of harpoon. I feel happy. People will eat."

Paul drew in his breath. "Man, what a way to live!"

Great-grandfather shook his head. "Good times and bad times in old days, Kabloona. These days we are not hungry and there is help when we are sick. But — old days was good too."

No one spoke for several seconds, then John said, "There is more to the story. Tell us the rest."

The old man's face grew sad. "Maybe is better to stop now."

"Tell us," Paul begged.

Willard, Wallace, Grandfather, Joe and Sam silently scanned the water for whales. Though they had heard the old man's story before, they listened politely.

"How about Kiogiak? Did he get a seal, too?" Paul asked.

Great-grandfather nodded. "He get seal."

"Man! It would be great to bring a seal home when your people were starving!" Paul said to Charles and John.

"Yeah," they murmured quietly.

"Kiogiak was Nasarlulik's only son. Kiogiak learn fast. Our people know he is leader. We hoped one time he would use his good mind to guide us."

"Tell us about his getting the seal," Paul urged.

"I not see or hear Kiogiak," Great-grandfather began. "I think I will wait by breathing hole 'til Nasarlulik come, then we go to Kiogiak and we go home together. I think no more seal come to hole where I have chopped ice away. They know it is not same, but I wait. Was cold — maybe forty below zero. I sit down on snow block with harpoon. Soon I hear it — the sound of seal at breathing hole. But this one not same. He is not careful. Was easy to drive harpoon into head of seal. I start pull him out. Was heavy — more heavy than first seal and he fight hard. I slip and almost fall into hole. Then I get him out." The old man hesitated.

After a time he went on, speaking slowly. "There is another harpoon head in seal's back, and thong

hangs through breathing hole under ice.   I pull.
Then I see why is so heavy.   Kiogiak is fast in
line.   Seal had pull him under ice."

"That's terrible!" Paul said.

"Was bad — very bad," Great-grandfather replied.
After a moment he said, "We have plenty food now but
there is sadness in Inuit houses.   People loved
Kiogiak."

They were silent.   After a time Sam got up.   "We
go back to camp.   No more whales today."

Soon they were aboard the **Tuk** chugging back toward whale camp.   Paul was unable to put the story
of Kiogiak from his mind.   Charles and John were
quiet.   Finally John said, "I'll write the story of
Kiogiak.   When I'm home at Tuk I'll make notes so I
won't forget.   Someday when I have more education I
will put the story in a book with the other stories
Great-grandfather has told about the old days.   He
may not be here then but I will remember the things
he says.   It will help us to remember the ways of
the past and that we must work together or something
bad will happen to us."

"I believe it," Charles said quietly.   "I read
somewhere that we Inuit live with one foot in the
past and one in the present."

Paul smiled, "We'd say you have one foot on a
banana peel."

"That about says it," John laughed.

The next morning the water was clear and sparkling.   Joe watched for whales from the bluff.   Sud-

denly he shouted, "Whales! Whales blowing to the southwest!" In the matter of a few minutes the men were in the schooner and on their way.

Soon John shouted, "Grandfather Katoayak's boat has stopped!"

"We wait. Soon he get engine going," Grandfather Nigiyak said shutting off the **Tuk**'s engine. The old schooner bobbed within shouting distance of the **Aklavik**.

"You not wait, Silas!" Grandfather Katoayak called. "Whales be gone soon!"

"We wait!" the call went across the sparkling water. The third boat continued on its way to the southwest. As the sound of the engine faded away, a low drone took its place.

"Airplane!" Willard's voice showed his displeasure.

Sam came from below deck. "She's leaking bad," he commented.

"Some day we fix her little bit," Grandfather said with no sign of concern.

Wallace looked angry. "I knew it! That plane is flying low over the water!"

Sam muttered, "No whale hunting today. We go back to camp when Ishmael gets motor started."

Grandfather stared to the southwest where an approaching red, black and white Twin Otter float plane flew low above the water.

Wallace snorted, "Tourists! They want to see whales! They drive them away and scare the ducks and swans off their nests!"

The plane dipped its wings as it roared above them. No one waved from the boats below. Above, faces were pressed to the plane windows, all searching for a closer view of the Arctic waters, the hunting Eskimos and animals of the tundra.

The crew of the **Tuk** were silent. At last Paul said, "Maybe there will be more whales later."

Great-grandfather said softly, "Not today, but some day we get whales so young men know how."

All at once the motor of the **Aklavik** barked sharply. A cheer went up from the crew. She pulled alongside the **Tuk**.

"We go back to camp," Grandfather Katoayak called.

"Could go on shore and put out nets. Many fish here," Joe shouted.

A few minutes later as they were placing the nets, the **Inuvik** returned. The crew reported that they had not seen whales. Late that afternoon the three boats returned to camp with a large catch of fish. The women and girls cleaned and filleted the fish which were hung to dry high on driftwood poles out of the reach of the dogs.

During the next several days the cold north wind was too strong to go out on the choppy waters between the islands. The two following windless days when the water was calm, the lookout on the bluff did not see any whales.

Finally when Paul began to think he might not see

a whale hunt, the call came from Grandfather Katoayak on the bluff that he had sighted whales.
Quickly the old unseaworthy schooners were manned
and the ancient one-cylinder inboard engines, each
with its own characteristic put-put, labored through
the waves.

Everything was ready including the 30-30 and .303
Enfield rifles, and the harpoons with detachable
bronze pointed ends which were attached to a one-
fourth inch line about forty feet long. The other
end of the line was fastened to a sealed empty oil
drum with about half the line wound around it. The
rest of the line was coiled on deck so it could
unwind easily.

Excitement was high for the general feeling was
that this day they would be successful in the hunt.
Suddenly, dead ahead several whales surfaced to
blow. The puffs of condensed moisture rose into the
clear cool air.

Grandfather called to Willard who was steering
the boat. "Don't get close to them! Stay twenty
yards behind!"

Great-grandfather explained to the young men,
"Too close, they turn fast — get away before boat
turns around."

The other two schooners were not far away. Every
man was intent on the whales ahead. Sam and Grandfather held rifles while Joe and Wallace grasped
harpoons. Great-grandfather, John and Paul watched.

"Now!" Great-grandfather shouted as a pure white

whale about fifteen feet long surfaced in the ten foot deep water. Sam's and Grandfather's rifles rang out. The whale lunged as the **Tuk** drew near. Joe, poised and ready with the harpoon, waited until the boat was close to the floundering whale. Then, with deadly accuracy, he plunged the harpoon into the snow-white animal, and Great-grandfather tossed the sealed oil drum overboard. Everyone cheered.

Paul pointed to the **Aklavik.** "They got one too!"

Grandfather Katoayak waved. The **Inuvik,** to the left of the others still pursued a fast swimming whale. Willard accelerated the motor and they sped toward a second spouting whale.

"When will we get the one we killed?" John asked.

"The oil drum floats. We get her on way back," Great-grandfather said. "Maybe we get another."

Wallace hurried to take over the steering from his brother who grabbed the rifle Grandfather thrust at him. Sam handed his rifle to Charles. They followed the whale for a few minutes, knowing that soon she must come up to breathe. Then, there it was, the telltale spurt of water and condensed moisture. Charles and Willard raised their rifles, aimed at the bit of white head above the water, and fired.

"She's hit!" John shouted as the animal thrashed about in the water.

Wallace pulled the **Tuk** as close to the fighting whale as he could. Sam, with harpoon ready, waited. Then with great power he thrust the harpoon into the whale's back.

"She's still fighting," Paul said.

"Shoot another bullet into her head!" Grandfather yelled.

Willard and Charles fired again and the big animal began to sink. Someone shouted, "Throw out the drum!"

Paul, being near the large can, tossed it overboard. "Your foot!" John yelled as Paul felt the painful jerk of the rapidly tightening line about his left leg above his boot top. Frantically he tried to loosen it as he was dragged toward the edge of the boat by the sinking whale.

With lightning speed Sam and Grandfather grabbed him about the waist and dragged him back. Charles, John and Great-grandfather frantically unwound the coil of line in an attempt to provide slack rope.

Paul thought his leg would be pulled from his body as the line cut viciously into his flesh. Sam and Grandfather, their arms locked about his waist in a vise-like grip kept shouting, "Cut line! Cut line!" The whale surfaced briefly in her death struggle, and in that split second the line slackened and John slipped the loop over Paul's extended leg.

"The whale!" he gasped. "Don't let her get away!"

The oil drum bobbed a short distance behind them. "She not get away," Grandfather said.

The concerned crew gathered about Paul who sat on

a five gallon oil can. "Your leg is all right?" Grandfather asked.

Paul pulled up his jeans. An angry purplish rope burn ringed the calf of his leg. "It smarts a little," he said pulling his pant leg down, "but I'm lucky. I thought I was going to the bottom with the whale."

Great-grandfather nodded. "Many Inuit men die that way."

"I'm glad you didn't have to cut the line because you'd have lost the whale," Paul said, gingerly testing his weight on the left leg. Pains shot through his hip.

Watching him, Sam remarked, "It hurts for few days."

"Yeah." He hobbled about. "I can walk so nothing's broken." He looked at the concerned faces about him. "Thanks," he said. "I was stupid to get tangled in the line."

Sam shrugged. "That's whale hunting."

An hour later when they had not sighted more whales, the three old schooners returned to collect the dead animals. The floating cans marked the spot where each whale was to be found.

"How do we get them on board?" Paul asked as they pulled along beside the first oil drum.

Joe reached for the rope on the drum, pulled it aboard and fastened the line securely. "We pull them behind boat," he replied.

On the way back to camp there was much laughing

and joking. Two beluga trailed behind the **Tuk**, and one each was towed by the other two boats.

Back in camp at the island cove an excited group of women and children waited as the whales were pulled up on the beach at the south end of camp.

While the hunters ate, laughed and joked, the women's work began. With their crescent-shaped ulus they first severed the whale's head with a crosswise cut. Paul watched while he drank tea and ate bannock and jam. The women rapidly slashed the trunk of the animal into two round pieces and a tail section.

Billy and the girls stood watching. Grandmother Katoayak trimmed strips from the tail of the sixteen foot animal and gave one to Billy, Margaret and Agnes. She motioned, smiling as she indicated that they should eat.

"It's raw!" Margaret exclaimed.

The women laughed. Grandmother Katoayak munched a piece of the meat with great relish.

"Try it," Annie said to Agnes. "It's good."

Reluctantly Margaret nibbled a bit of the meat. The others watched as she took a second and third bite. "I like it," she said.

Soon everyone in camp was chewing a strip of the raw beluga tail which for hundreds of years had been considered a rare delicacy by Eskimo whale hunters. Paul held a strip of the meat in his hand as he watched his friends. He didn't like rare hamburgers. His stomach twisted at the thought of eating this raw meat.   Though no one said anything, he knew they were watching.

Gingerly he nibbled a bit of the meat.   It was cool with a flavor different from anything he had ever tasted.   After three or four bites he lost his aversion to the thoughts of raw meat and in a short time he was munching with enjoyment the last of his strip of beluga tail.

Great-grandfather chuckled.   "Kabloona, you make good Inuit."

"I almost wish I were Inuit," Paul answered.   "I like the way you live."   No one spoke but Sam and Grandfather nodded in agreement.

The women again were hard at work.   Margaret and Agnes helped cut up the meat which was rinsed in the sea and laid on the grass.   Paul was fascinated at the speed with which the women worked, their ulus flashing in the sunlight.   After an hour one whale was completely cut up.   Without resting they set to work on the second animal.   When it was cut into two cylindrical pieces plus the head and tail sections, three or four inch thick layers of skin and under-lying blubber were peeled from the trunk.   The meat along the backbone was removed in large chunks.

The women chatted in Inutitut as they worked, occasionally tossing pieces of blubber and bones to the circle of waiting dogs.   The viscera were thrown into the water where they eventually would wash away.   The kidneys and brains were set aside to be eaten in camp.   The long whale stomachs were emptied by the girls and rinsed in water.

"What will you do with those?" Paul asked Grandfather as he watched the girls blow up the stomachs and tie the ends with a thong.

Grandfather sipped his tea slowly before he answered. "We let air out when skin is dry. Whale stomach make good bag for store food in."

The women worked on. The large skin and blubber pieces were cut in zig-zag fashion and hung on poles, out of the dogs' reach, to dry for two or three days.

Clothes which the women had washed earlier in the day flapped in the wind on lines strung beside the white muslin tents. Paul exercised his aching hip by walking until the pain lessened. Then, helping himself to more tea he sat beside John who was talking to Grandfather Katoayak in Inutitut. Billy came to join in the conversation.

As the women and girls bent over the whale carcasses wisps of dark hair whipped across their faces. Paul thought again as he had many times this summer that it was beautiful how well the group got along. Though no one person was in charge of organizing the camp, each one did his share of the work with no arguments or complaints. He thought of the Detroit area with its labor strikes, crime and unrest, and once again he hoped that the white man's modern progress would not destroy the Eskimo way of life.

"Would you like to, Paul?" John asked.

Paul started. "Huh?"

John laughed. "Grandfather Katoayak wants you, Billy, Margaret and I to live in his tent the rest of the time in camp."

"I'd like that," Paul said wondering how he would communicate with Grandmother Katoayak.

Ishmael Katoayak smiled, his wrinkled brown face showing his pleasure. "Ella and me, we want to know our son's children and their friend, Kabloona." He motioned toward Paul.

When the women had the whale skin and blubber drying they stopped work and gathered in the Katoayak tent for the midnight meal. The sleeping platform of fur and fabric blankets was at the back, the sheet metal stove near the front and a few boxes of provisions and supplies were piled at the side of the tent which was almost identical to that of Grandfather and Grandmother Nigiyak. Most of the conversation during the meal was in Inutitut. Paul thought that since they had arrived at whale camp both adults and children were rapidly returning to their original language.

After a time Grandfather Nigiyak said, "Ishmael, tell young folks about when you and Abel got in blizzard near Tuk."

The old man sipped his tea as he looked at Paul. "Kabloona, I talk English so you know how it was long time ago." He settled back and began the story. "We grow up near Tuk, brother Abel and me. Abel was twenty year old. I was eighteen. In

November we go to traps with dog team. It was nice day, not cold. We go to traps and then make little igloo near shore. While we sleep, west wind come. I wake up wet. Bed is in water. I wake Abel. His bed is wet too. Wind blow hard and drive water on top of ice. We hurry and dress. My pants are wet. I cannot find socks. Abel give me his second pair pants that was shoved in top of igloo to block the kringak."

John whispered to Paul, "The smoke hole."

Grandfather Katoayak continued. "While I dress, Abel make hole in igloo wall and crawl out. We start to the land. Storm is bad. We are afraid to leave everything. We cannot live in storm without supplies. We go back to flooded igloo and cover up with piece of wet tarpaulin and blanket. Snow is blow all over outside. We cannot see through it. Wind is blow so hard we cannot build dry igloo. We dig hole in snow and crawl in. Wind blow snow away from us. Clothes are wet. Are very cold. Wind is like — what you say — like gale. We cannot travel. No place to go for us. We wrap up in wet tarpaulin and blanket and try sleep on snow for many hours. Are cold and cannot sleep." He paused.

A wolf howled forlornly in the distance. The dogs began to bark. Great-grandfather cupped his tea mug in his hands and looked with pleasure at the interested faces of the young people. "Good," he murmured. "They not forget."

"Why didn't you freeze to death?" Margaret asked.

"Sila is sometimes bad, sometimes good," Grandfather Nigiyak said slowly.

"What is sila?" Paul asked.

"Weather," Grandfather Katoayak said. "After long time the wind stops. We hurry to build igloo. Abel stuff his caribou parka in smoke hole and we roll up in wet blanket. Wind howled again. We hear noise made by water. We think ice will break under igloo. Two days we are cold in igloo without sleep."

LURE OF THE ARCTIC

"Why didn't you go to shore and build an igloo?" John asked.

"Not much snow on land. Only snow on ice near shore where there was snowbank beside pressure ridge. After two days, wind stop. We think dogs are washed away by tide. We go out. Dogs are alive, all but two. Our sled is covered with water and ice. We break ice with knives and pull out sled and dogs' harness.

"Abel's parka is spoiled by water when he plug hole in igloo. It is froze stiff. Blanket not warm like parka. We know there is old cabin two miles away. We go there while wind is quiet. We are glad to dry clothes there and we sleep. My feet froze after I lost socks in wet igloo.

"When clothes are dry we harness dogs to sled. I cannot walk far on froze feet. I ride on sled and Abel wrap me in blanket. In two days we are at Tuk."

"Father and Mother glad to see us. They think we are froze to death. Eight days we are gone. Was good to be home."

Great-grandfather said softly, "Sila makes life hard for Inuit in old times."

"Did freezing your feet make you limp after that?" Billy asked.

"Yes. Feet was bad. Toes get black. The shaman, Savgut, try drive out evil spirit from toes. In trance he squat down on floor. He call on good spirits for help. Abel, father, mother, friends all

143

watch Savgut while he talk with spirits. We not know this talk he says. Spirits tell shaman he must cut off toes. Toes are dead. Shaman cut toes off. Feet get better."

Billy's eyes were huge. "Did he cut off all your toes?"

"I show you." Grandfather Katoayak pulled off his boots and socks. No toes remained on the stumpy right foot and only two smaller ones had been spared on the left. Billy shuddered.

"My feet scare you?" Grandfather asked. "Savgut save my life. I had what we call gangrene. Good spirits tell Savgut to cut off toes that have evil spirit in them and throw them in sea. He chop hole in ice and throw dead toes in water. Feet are better then."

Paul noticed the glances that passed between Willard, Wallace, Charles and John before they stared silently at the floor of the tent. A tiny smile tugged at the corners of Margaret's mouth. Only Billy, of the young people, believed in evil spirits and the power of the shaman. Yet no one had laughed or ridiculed the beliefs of the older generation.

A moment of silence followed the completion of the story. Then John said, "Thank you, Grandfather Katoayak, for telling us the story. When I get home I will write it down so I don't forget." The men nodded their approval.

For two days the little camp on Kendall Island was battered by the wind. The children played ring toss, searched for bird eggs and hunted ground squirrels with sling shots. Billy, Margaret and Agnes brought ten fat little animals to camp. Grandmother Katoayak taught Margaret and Agnes to skin and clean the animals, chatting with them in Inutitut as they worked.

"Let's chew the hides to make them soft like Grandmother Nigiyak showed us with the Arctic hare skins," Margaret suggested.

"Okay. Then this winter we will have soft skins and we can make things to sell to tourists next summer."

"Yeah!" Margaret exclaimed. "I want to get enough money so I can buy a little radio of my own."

"Me too," Agnes agreed tossing a skinned and cleaned ground squirrel into the kettle of water.

Grandmother Nigiyak squatted nearby. "Radio okay," she said. "T.V. no good for children."

"Grandma!" Margaret exclaimed. "We like T.V.! Why do you say it's no good?"

Susie Nigiyak spoke to Ella Katoayak in Inutitut. She nodded her agreement. Women from the other tents wandered in and out. Most of them spoke English. Paul, sitting with the card-playing men nearby, picked up bits of the women's conversation.

"Grandmothers see children sit in front of T.V. long time every day. They learn Kabloonat way. Fighting, drinking, killing. Children think that is way to live. Soon they think Inuit way is not good," Annie Olorgrak said.

Another woman joined in. "Is true, children. You stay up to watch T.V. and you are late for school in morning."

"But there are Inuit programs on T.V.," Agnes argued. "They even speak Inutitut."

The women nodded. "Few hours a week are for Inuit. Rest of programs all about Kabloonat cowboys, police and Indians," Annie added.

"Some Inuit spend money for T.V. set and family does not have things they need," Grandmother Nigiyak said. She shrugged. "But young people want T.V."

After the strips of whale skin and blubber had

LURE OF THE ARCTIC

cured in the sun for several days, the women cut
them into pieces about the size of a man's hand.
With their ulus they trimmed most of the blubber
from the skin and rendered it to whale oil by heating it in half of a fifty-five gallon oil drum over
a driftwood fire. The three-fourths inch thick
pieces of snow-white skin then were boiled in water
and preserved in assorted sizes of jars of whale
oil.

Paul watched the numerous operations with interest. "Is that whale skin good?" he asked Charles.

"It's muktuk," Charles answered. "Muktuk is good any time, but in winter it really tastes good. It's one of our best Inuit foods."

The women had cut the black whale meat into thin strips about half an inch thick and eight inches wide and thirty inches long. Part of these strips now swung from poles where it dried in the sun, and the rest hung inside a rough smoke house where it cured over a smoldering fire.

"This will be dried meat. It is hard and brittle and not easy to chew," John explained. "Great-grandfather doesn't eat mipku until it has been soaked in whale oil or boiled."

"Mipku?" Paul asked.

"Mipku is hard, black, dried whale meat, and muktuk is the soft, white whale skin. They both are good. But the whale flipper, after it's aged — that's something else!"

At last the wind died away and the cry of "Whales!" came from the lookout behind the camp. Within minutes the old schooners were on the way. John and Paul went on the **Aklavik** with Grandfather Katoayak and his crew.

Like the **Tuk**, the **Aklavik** leaked badly. As he bailed and watched water seep into the old boat Paul wondered again why his friends didn't repair the boats during the long days in camp when they were unable to go whaling. The laughter on deck above him was loud and boisterous. He bailed on.

"I'll take over." John, unobserved, had been watching his friend. "What are you thinking about?" He took the pail and began the rhythmic bailing.

"I was wondering why the men don't repair the boats so they don't leak."

John broke the bailing rhythm for a moment. He looked puzzled. "The boats are all right," he said. "Whaling boats always leak."

Paul dropped the subject. It's a difference in our cultures, he thought. He doesn't understand.

A half hour later Paul stood near John and Grandfather Katoayak on the deck of the **Aklavik** to watch. Each held his rifle at ready. Jim Tautu steered the boat behind a fast swimming whale.

"Now!" Grandfather shouted as the whale surfaced.

The two rifles barked as one and the whale disappeared. Jim accelerated the motor and sped toward the spot where they had last seen the whale.

"Did you miss her?" Paul asked.

"Don't know," Grandfather replied.

All eyes searched the water. "There!" Paul shouted. She is lying on the bottom! How can we get her?"

The motor slowed. Through the clear twelve-foot-deep water the still white shape of the whale could be seen.

"She's dead." Grandfather reached for a large grappling hook attached to a long line. He threw the hook overboard at the side of the dead whale and motioned for the boat to go ahead. Slowly they dragged the hook back and forth over the spot where the whale could be seen. Finally after many tries, the line tightened.

"Got her!" John shouted as the white body began to rise to the surface. He and Paul raced to the back of the boat. Grandfather and his friend Philip Adjick were pulling in the line. When the beluga was at the surface Philip exclaimed, "See why she sink? Two bullet holes in head! Good shots!"

Grandfather smiled and patted John's shoulder. "Like father when he was boy. Was good shot too. Both my boys, Joe in **Inuvik** and Jack in **Tuk**, they was good hunters. Now they work on docks." There was a note of sadness in his voice.

Only one whale was taken that day by the hunters. Back at camp the women and girls had it cut up in a short time.

Sitting inside the Katoayak tent that night, Great-grandfather Nigiyak said, "Soon we go home."

"Do we have enough whale meat?" Billy asked.

"The **Aklavik** has two, the **Tuk** has two and with the one the **Inuvik** had when we got to camp, they have two," Willard said.

"Is enough," Grandfather Nigiyak said. "We not kill more than we need."

"What is the date?" Paul asked.

Wallace looked at the tiny calendar on his watch band. "July 28," he replied.

Billy grinned, "July 28, 1975," he said.

Paul said, "By a month from now I'll be back in

Detroit getting ready to go to the university." He hesitated. "I wish there was work here in the winter for my father and me. I'd like to spend a winter here."

Willard shook his head. "Winter is a bad time. Forty — sixty below zero. Wind — snow — and many days with no daylight. You'd do better to be at college."

Grandfather Katoayak spoke to Grandfather Nigiyak. "Silas, I like John and Kabloona to go home with us for a few days."

"To Aklavik?" John asked. "How would we get back to Tuk?"

The old man smiled. "Walter Maniksak take you back in plane. He come to Aklavik."

John looked at Grandfather Nigiyak. "What do you think? It costs a lot to fly. I don't have much money."

Grandfather nodded. "I know, but your father like you visit where he live when he is little boy. He pay for you."

John turned to Paul. "Would you want to do it?"

"You bet! How long before we'd be back at Tuk?"

Grandfather Katoayak puffed on his pipe. "Two, three weeks," he said.

"Man, that's great! Thanks for asking me!" Paul exclaimed, silently thinking that the grandmothers had not been included in the decision. On several other occasions he had noticed that the women were expected to agree with whatever decision was made by the men.

As soon as the whale meat strips of mipku were dry and the smoked meat was cured, it was evenly divided and packed along with many jars of muktuk, for the homeward journey.

As they loaded the barge at 1 A.M. on August 4, Paul paused to enjoy the beauty of the clouds in the Arctic sky. There was the orange-red sun a few degrees above the horizon, the wild splendor of flaming colors of crimson, gold, orange and coral which blended into pink and violet, while overhead there was the dark blue dome of the heavens. Paul wanted to take in every detail of the spectacular.

"Pretty, yes Kabloona?" Great-grandfather asked.

Paul nodded. "I want to always remember how it is here."

"I'll remember, too," Margaret said. "When I am home I will make pictures of the sky and of the things we did in whale camp."

Agnes said, "You make good pictures. Maybe someday you'll be a famous Inuit artist."

"I like to draw pictures. I'd like to show the things we did at whale camp. And I want to make pictures of things that happened in the stories our grandfathers tell us. John will write the stories and I'll make the pictures."

Great-grandfather smiled his approval of the plan.

That morning by eleven o'clock the **Aklavik** was ready to leave. Goodbyes were said and Grandfather

Nigiyak promised to tell Paul's father of the change in plans.

Grandfather Katoayak said, "Silas and Susie, they will have fine time in Aklavik." He nodded toward John and Paul. He limped to the side of the old schooner for a last word with friends on shore.

Everyone waved as the battered old schooner with its leaky barge pulled away from shore and started across Mackenzie Bay. They had started the trip to the little inland settlement of Aklavik.

Soon the remaining people at whale camp would be leaving for Tuktoyaktuk. Kendall Island would be deserted for another year except for an occasional hunter or trapper.

AKLAVIK

Life aboard the **Aklavik** was much the same as on the **Tuk.** Dogs and humans shared the space that was not taken by tents, supplies and muktuk and mipku. Because the boat was going upstream, progress was slow. Almost as soon as they were out of sight of the people on Kendall Island the card game started. Since the five other men were of Grandfather Kato-ayak's age, most of the conversation was in Inuti-tut.

John and Paul were included in the card games and as an incentive to win, the loser of a hand must bail fifty pails of water from the leaky boat. While the men laughed, talked and played cards the women sat on oil drums with parka hoods up and their

154

backs to the northwest wind as they chatted in Inutitut.

That evening after camp was pitched in a cove on the shore of Mackenzie Bay fish nets were set out. Paul and John picked a pail of bright yellow berries which the Inuit people called akpiks.

As they sat inside the tent of Jim and Nellie Tantu for the evening meal of fish, bannock, akpiks and tea, Paul tried to understand the discussion. Finally he whispered to John, "What are they talking about?"

"They want to stay over a day to pick akpiks."

The next day Grandmother Katoayak and her friends Nellie Tantu, Sophie Adjuk, Mary Kaludjak, Martha Tiktak and Sata Nowdluk picked many quarts of the raspberry-like berries. They also found a quantity of vitamin C-rich rose hips, which are the seed berry of the wild roses that grow almost everywhere during the short Arctic summer.

Walking over the tundra in sixty degree weather among waving fur-like white cotton grass, daisies, wild roses and low berry laden bushes, Paul found it hard to believe that in a few short weeks this land would be in the grip of another howling Arctic winter. Daydreaming, he was startled by John's sharp command. "Look!"

Standing in the water of a nearby tundra lake was a cow moose and two calves. Without moving the young men watched as the mother plunged her nose deep into the water to pull up great mouthfuls of

tender plants. The calves pastured in shallow water near the edge of the lake. At last the animals trotted away.

"We don't see many moose near Tuk now," John said.

Back at camp they told of seeing the moose and her calves. "We could have shot her easy if we'd had a rifle," John said.

Elijah Tiktak shook his head. "Babies need

mother."

"We not need meat," Philip Adjuk added.

"In Aklavik we hunt moose September and October," Simon Kaludjak explained.

Grandfather Katoayak limped over to fill his tea mug. "September, October. Law say we can hunt bull and cow. We try then."

The women returned to camp with buckets of ak-piks. Their facial expressions showed happiness. Paul watched as they chatted and packed layers of berries between layers of sugar in the dried whales' stomachs until the balloon-like containers were filled.

Grandmother Katoayak smiled at Paul's interest and said something to John who relayed the message. "She says this jam will taste good in the winter." Paul grinned and nodded.

At the evening meal Mary Kaludjak indicated to Paul by gestures that the pot of food she was serving was a special treat. The older men already were smacking their lips with enjoyment. After he got a whiff of the odor from the pot, Paul took only a small piece. "What is it?" he said to John putting the tidbit into his mouth.

"Rotten whale flipper," John replied as he declined the strong smelling delicacy which Mary held before him.

Paul swallowed and choked. The middle aged Eskimos laughed loudly, smacking their lips to show their enjoyment of the whale flipper which smelled like Limburger cheese. "Whale flipper tasted good when it was fresh," he said to John.

"Yeah, but this is rotten. Last year some people in Tuk got botulism from eating it."

Next morning a cold heavy fog hung over the water. The wet air penetrated the muslin tents like rain. The men delayed leaving until mid-afternoon when the fog lifted. Then, because the water was coming into the boat faster than it could be bailed out, the schooner was run aground and the leak repaired just enough to keep the bailers busy and to provide an incentive for the card game.

A few days later after the long trip from Kendall Island was at an end the whale hunters finally arrived at Aklavik. They were welcomed by relatives and children who shouted greetings. Teenagers pushed and wrestled, adults called and dogs barked and ran to meet old canine acquaintances.

South of the tree line, the small settlement was built on flat land only a few feet above the water level of the surrounding delta. Trees grew along the banks of the Peel Channel, willows, alders, balsam, poplar and small black spruce.

Paul silently compared the appearance of Aklavik and Tuk. In Tuk there were no trees. In population, Aklavik was slightly larger. The homes were similar, some made of logs, some of painted wood siding, others of asbestos shingle and a few of the more recent were of painted aluminum. Most of the homes were small one story buildings, but an occasional house had one or two low attic rooms. The blue modern-looking school and the pink hospital were identical to those built by the government in Tuk. White fuel oil tanks beside each building, discarded freezers and refrigerators, furniture and rusty barrels in yards, an occasional pickup in the drive and beside most homes there were one or two snowmobiles; a visual survey told Paul something of the people's way of life.

The stores were few. A low gold and turquoise colored Hudson's Bay Company store, a small grocery, a garage and the Aklavik Fur Garment Co-op were the leading places of business.

Carrying their sleeping bags and bundles of clothing, Paul and John went with John's grandparents to their home.

"Did you live here when my father was small?" John asked looking about the tiny house at the worn furniture.

"Yes," Grandfather said, "but my boys want make money so they go to Inuvik and Tuk. They like better than trapping." He looked out over the waters of the delta.

"My father still hunts and traps near Tuk and so does Uncle Joe at Inuvik," John argued.

Grandfather nodded. "Not like when I was young man. They work on dock in summer for Kabloonat. They forget Inuit life. They like Kabloonat money."

After the evening meal at the oilcloth-covered kitchen table the young men walked around the settlement. Behind many homes fish were drying on wooden racks out of the reach of dogs, and various kinds of skins hung on lines near the houses.

"Caribou hides," John said, "and that big one there near the church is a grizzly."

"Yeah?"

"Yeah. My father says there are grizzlies in the foothills of the Richardson Mountains over there to the south and west of Aklavik." They looked toward the sun which hung above the rough hilly country a few miles away.

Hearing shouts, they hurried to investigate. A baseball game was in progress. "Hi!" the teenage pitcher shouted. "You fellows want to play?"

"Yeah!" they both called.

"We need a fielder and a pitcher. Can either of you pitch?"

"I can," Paul answered.

"Good. We need a pitcher on my team."

Someone threw Paul a glove and he ran to his position. A stocky muscular boy stood at the plate, bat in hand.

"Watch out for Tony!" the center fielder shouted to Paul. "He hits to left field and he's got on base three times tonight!"

Paul went into his windup and the ball sailed over the outside corner of the plate. Tony swung. The ball smacked into the catcher's mitt.

"Strike one!" the umpire shouted.

Again Paul went into his windup and again Tony

swung.

"Strike two!" the umpire called.

Paul took a deep breath as he watched for the catcher's sign. The third ball was knee high directly over the heart of the plate. Tony swung.

"Strike three!" the umpire said. Tony hung his head as he went to the bench.

"Great pitching!" the catcher shouted to Paul.

A few innings later Paul said to John, "This is fun. I didn't know how much I'd missed baseball until tonight."

"You play on a team in Detroit?"

"I started in Little League when I was eight, but I haven't played much since I was out of high school two years ago."

When the game was over the players gathered around John and Paul who explained how they happened to be in Aklavik. At twelve o'clock they headed back to Grandfather Katoayak's home for a snack before bedtime. Children still were playing outside when they finally went to bed.

Except for people who worked in places of business, Aklavik's residents slept late. When John and Paul went outside after breakfast at eleven o'clock there were few people about.

"It's quiet," Paul commented, "like Tuk is in the forenoon." He kicked a beer can into the weeds beside the board sidewalk.

"When kids don't have to go to school, they sleep late. Their mothers sleep late too. There aren't

Inuit grandmother in summer parka

any roads outside the settlement so there's no place to drive cars. In winter when the delta is frozen we travel on winter roads in Skidoos, cars and trucks."

"Where is there to go?"

"We can travel between Tuk and Inuvik and Akla-

vik. There are winter roads all the way to Yellowknife."

"How come you have never been to Aklavik if you
could go in the winter?" Paul asked.

"It's a long ways to Aklavik and I've been in
school. My father is busy with his trap line."
John reached down to pet a dog that nuzzled his
hand.

They glanced up at the sound of an approaching
plane, then walked rapidly toward the channel where
the Cessna float plane was circling in preparation
for landing. As they reached the water's edge the
plane touched down in the water, settled and taxied
to the wooden dock. Five passengers climbed down
aided by the pilot who already was on the dock.

"Who are they?" Paul said softly as two middle
aged women and three men walked down the dock toward
the dusty runway where land planes came in.

"Tourists," John replied. "We left for whale
camp before they had started to come to Tuk."

A small land plane approached the settlement from
the east. The first group of people waited with the
pilot as the second plane, a five passenger Piper
Aztec, touched down on the gravel runway stirring up
a dense cloud of dust with its wheels and propeller.

"More tourists," Paul said as four elderly women
were helped from the plane. They were about the age
of his grandmother. The two groups of people
joined.

"Wasn't that a nice flight from Inuvik?" a woman

asked a friend from the first group.

"I got some beautiful pictures of the delta," the second woman replied. "We were low enough so I took pictures of an oil drilling outfit and a barge loaded with crude oil."

"I'd hate to be on a plane that had to land out there," one of the men commented, motioning to the east.

"I'd figure it was curtains," the other man added. "Many planes lost up here?" he asked the pilot.

The bearded young man with bushy hair stooped to roll his rubber boots another fold below his faded jeans. He hesitated a moment as he took off his red and black plaid jacket. "A few," he replied shortly. "We'll be leaving for Inuvik at one thirty." He tossed his jacket into the plane and strode toward the business section of town.

"Harry!" one of the women called. "Do you know where we should go?"

The only young man in the group, a six-foot, four-inch blond man, smiled pleasantly at the middle aged and elderly people. "We'll go as a group now, then later you can wander around on your own until plane time. Just be sure to be back at one thirty."

"He's the tour director," John said to Paul as the tourists followed the young man down the dirt road which circled the settlement.

"Let's go with them," Paul suggested. "Maybe we can learn more about Aklavik."

LURE OF THE ARCTIC

Harry led the way, stopping to explain as questions were asked. "Aklavik has a population of seven hundred sixty people," the tour director began. "The name, Aklavik, is Eskimo for 'place of the barren grizzly bear.' This is an old settlement. Anglican and Roman Catholic missions were set up in 1918. The Royal Canadian Mounted Police post was established in 1922. The Hudson's Bay Company store opened in 1926. So you can see why Aklavik became the chief center of the Mackenzie delta, for Inuvik was not started until the 1960s.

"In the early days the population was about evenly divided between Eskimos and Indians, with a few whites. The population grew due to the expansion of the Anglican and Roman Catholic hospitals and residential schools. Because of this concentration of activities and schools, the government opened administrative offices here for the region. By 1952 Aklavik and the surrounding region had a population of 1556."

"What happened? Why did half of the people leave?" a man asked.

"Aklavik floods because the land is low. The federal government decided to build a modern administrative center for the area in the early 1960s. For various reasons, one of them being the frequent flooding of Aklavik, the site of Inuvik was chosen. Many Eskimos and Indians, most of them young people, moved to Inuvik. Many have remained there but some have returned to the life of their ancestors in the

Aklavik area."

John whispered, "My uncle is one who stayed in Inuvik. My father says Aklavik is a sea of mud in the spring. He calls it 'the mudtropolis of the North'." He chuckled.

The tour guide continued. "The main work here and in the surrounding area is fur trapping. Muskrats are the chief catch, though other fur bearing animals such as fox, lynx and wolverine are taken. Beaver pelts also are an important source of income. Caribou and an occasional moose are a source of meat. The native people also eat muskrats. In spring and summer some of them go to muskrat camps and later they may go to fish and whale camps. The native people say game, fish and fur-bearing animals are not as plentiful as they once were. They feel the white man is responsible for the decrease in wildlife due to water pollution caused by oil drilling and air traffic which frightens animals and birds from the area."

As the group moved on, Harry waited until John and Paul caught up to him. "Hi!" he greeted them. "I'm Harry Enlund, tour guide from Toronto."

Paul said, "This is my friend John Katoayak from Tuktoyaktuk, and I'm Paul Douglas from Detroit." He explained briefly how they happened to be in Aklavik. "Do you mind if we tag along with your group and listen?"

"Glad to have you."

At the next stop Harry explained why there were

few paved roads in the Arctic. Later he introduced John and Paul to the group. "Mr. Ritter, you and Paul may be neighbors in Michigan. He's from Detroit."

"He is? I'm from Farmington Hills. That's a suburb of Detroit," he explained.

Paul's eyes sparkled. "We are neighbors — almost. Farmington Hills is about twelve miles from where I live on the west side of the city." In the same breath he asked, "How are the Tigers doing?"

"They're in second place and gaining on the Yankees. If they don't go into a slump or have too many injuries, they might make it to the World Series."

"Wow!" Paul exclaimed. "That's great!"

The group moved on to the Hudson's Bay Company store with its miscellany of merchandise. While the women shopped, John said to Paul, "What are the Tigers and Yankees?"

"Baseball teams. The Detroit Tigers and New York Yankees. Man, if only the Tigers could keep winning maybe I'd get to see a World Series game at Tiger Stadium!"

Harry came to wait with the young men. "We're going to Tuk tomorrow if the weather is good," he said. "We will go to the docks, and I'd be glad to take a note from you to your father, if you'd like me to."

"That's great — only I don't have a pencil or paper," Paul said.

Harry took a notebook and pen from his pocket.

LURE OF THE ARCTIC

"Maybe you can write it while the ladies are shopping."

Paul rested the paper on top of a pile of shoe boxes. Hurriedly he dashed off this note:

Aklavik, N.W.T
August 12, 1975

Dear Dad,

John and I are having a fine time with his grandparents. We will be back in Tuk as soon as Walter Maniksak comes to pick us up.

Whale hunting was great. I wish you could have been with me.

After you read this note would you mail it to Mom and Carl and Karen so they'll know I'm okay? Thanks.

Your son,

Paul

From the Hudson's Bay Company store the tour group walked on past the grocery to the Fur Garment

Co-op building. Fireweed blossomed below the six narrow windows of the main workshop room. As they entered the low yellow building with the Canadian flag flying from its roof, a dark man appeared from the office on the right. He greeted Harry. "You have brought us more business?"

"Perhaps, if they like what they see."

"Look as long as you like," the manager said. "Our Co-op is operated by native labor. In the workroom you'll see items being made, and at the back in the room on the right there are many garments for sale. If you have questions, I'll be in the office."

In the workroom several women and two men were at work. The Eskimo men cut out garments from soft fur hides which lay stacked on a high work table. At a lower table before the windows four women sat as they sewed silky linings in fur jackets. They glanced up and smiled as several people snapped pictures.

Green cafe-type curtains shielded the tables from the midday sun. The women were short, dark, and to Paul, they appeared to be overweight. In the center of the room two young women in their early twenties worked at large electric sewing machines making slippers and mukluks. They seemed shy as though they disliked being observed. Several shelves were piled high with completed garments which had not been priced.

In the sales room racks were filled with jackets,

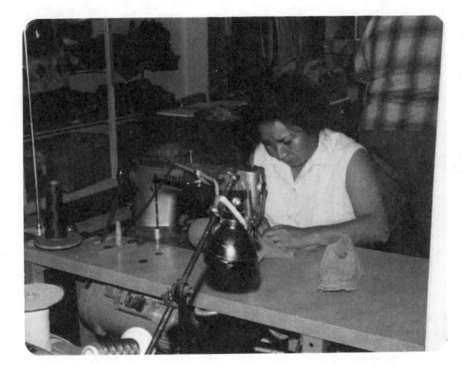

Woman making mukluks

coats and parkas, while shelf after shelf contained fur hats, caps, belts, slippers and mukluks.

Mr. Ritter bought a wolf-skin rug for his den, and a man and wife purchased fur hats. Two of the elderly ladies bought sealskin slippers for their grandchildren.

When they were outside the group strolled down the street past a low red asbestos-sided building with a small white sign above the door reading, "Aklavik Christian Assembly Church." White curtains hung at the front windows. Like all lawns in Akla-vik, the sparse grass was uncut.

As they turned in at the cemetery on the main street, Paul was aware of the contrasts in the various homes. On one side of the street there was a neat twenty by thirty foot log cabin with a wash-ing on the line. The shirts and dresses were bril-liantly clean and the white clothes sparkled. No junk littered the yard. The surrounding homes, some of them minus pieces of asbestos siding were less neat. Various pieces of discarded equipment lit-tered the yards. A bottled gas stove, a refrigera-tor lying on its side, a low table with one leg gone, a bicycle frame and several old boxes were visible to Paul in one quick glance.

He turned and walked rapidly to catch up with the group who were gathering beside a low white picket fence which enclosed a two-trunked tree stump with the letters "A.J." painted on it in white. Harry was talking.

"This is the grave of Albert Johnson, a white trapper. In 1931 two Royal Canadian Mounted Police constables were sent up the Rat River, which is south of Aklavik, to investigate complaints by the Loucheux Indians that their traps were being robbed by a white man named Albert Johnson.

"When the police reached Johnson's cabin, he refused to let them in so they came back to Aklavik to obtain a warrant for arrest from the commanding officer of the RCMP. Two more constables mushed back with the first two men to Johnson's cabin on the Rat River.

"When they tried to serve Johnson with the warrant, one of them, a man named King, was shot and wounded. The other three bundled King up and put him on a toboggan. It was forty-five degrees below zero but the Mounties returned to Aklavik, which was eighty miles away, in twenty hours. King underwent surgery and recovered.

"A special posse was assembled which included two men from Royal Canadian Corps of Signals, four trappers, four RCMP constables and Inspector Eames, who was in command of the expedition. They were well equipped with forty-two dogs pulling toboggans loaded with camp gear, bundles of dynamite, ammunition and a small arsenal of pistols, rifles and shotguns.

"The posse arrived at the mouth of the Rat River on January 9, 1932. During the battle which followed one of the trappers, Knut Lang, climbed on the roof of Johnson's cabin and set off a big charge of dynamite which opened up a hole in the thick frozen sod roof large enough to look through.

"The men were unable to enter the cabin due to Johnson's vicious assault, and they had to retreat to Aklavik. They left two men, a trapper Karl Gardlund and Constable Miller behind to watch Johnson. Yet, somehow he escaped, apparently without food or dogs.

"Later he was hunted down by Miller, Gardlund,

LURE OF THE ARCTIC

Sergeant Riddell and trapper Verville. In the attempted capture Johnson shot and killed Constable Miller. He then escaped to the Richardson Mountains west of Aklavik along the Yukon, Northwest Territories border.

"Inspector Eames requested air support from Fort McMurray where W. R. "Wop" May and his Junkers monoplane was stationed. It was three days before May could reach the place where Miller had been killed. ⁄The plane was used to track Johnson who covered his trail by traveling behind a migrating herd of caribou. He walked without snowshoes so that the animal tracks would cover his own.

"When they finally found him, Johnson shot and wounded Sergeant Hersey before being shot and killed himself at ten minutes past noon, February 17, 1932.

"The true identity of Albert Johnson has remained a mystery. All agree that he was a thief and a murderer. The newspapers called him "The Mad Trapper of Rat River." His body was flown here to Aklavik by Wop May for burial. His tombstone is this rotting tree stump with only the white painted letters "A. J." as an inscription. And so here in Aklavik ended the most famous manhunt the Canadian North has ever known."

"What a story!" Paul exclaimed.

Several of the tourists snapped pictures of Albert Johnson's grave as others wandered about the little cemetery. John and Paul stood by a gray marble marker atop a raised cement foundation. The grave was decorated with artificial flowers and a wreath that was covered with clear plastic attached to a wooden frame.

"Someone takes good care of the flowers on that grave," Paul commented. John's eyes went to the gravestone. "Look!" he exclaimed. "Karl Gardlund! Wasn't that one of the trappers who hunted Albert Johnson?"

"Yeah," Paul agreed. "It says 1906-1972. He would have been sixty-six years old when he died. Hey! Maybe Grandfather Katoayak knew him and Johnson, too!"

"Maybe. But my father and Uncle Joe were born in Tuk, so Grandfather wouldn't have been here in 1932 when Johnson was killed."

John and Paul thanked Harry for allowing them to stay with his group, and after saying goodbye, they started back to the Katoayak home. They could hear Harry saying, "We'll stop at the Anglican and Roman Catholic churches on the way back to the planes."

The settlement was quiet in the warm afternoon sun. A few adults were outside, and an occasional car stirred up the dust of the dirt street. Suddenly, a block away, the stillness was shattered by the staccato bark of a plane motor. Two or three minutes later the Piper Aztec climbed into the air above the treetops lining the Peel Channel, and shortly thereafter it was followed by the Cessna float plane. Shading their eyes against the sun, Paul and John watched.

LURE OF THE ARCTIC

"I wonder when Walter Maniksak will take us to Tuk? John said.

"Grandfather said he flies in here almost every week," Paul replied. "I hope he has his radio fixed. When Dad and I flew to Tuk with him, it wasn't working."

"He's a good pilot." John spoke with conviction.

That afternoon when lunch was finished Paul and the Katoayaks lingered at the table talking with Grandfather about Albert Johnson. "I know Gardlund. Good man, but they kill Johnson before my family come here," Grandfather said. "Bad man. Good he die. He steal and kill. People afraid of man like that."

"But Johnson was a white man," Paul said. "I haven't seen one of your people get angry. Don't you have trouble — disagreements?"

Grandfather smiled. "We learn — our grandfathers and great-grandfathers — that is bad for group when man or woman get angry. Bad temper, we are afraid of. Inuit say such man or woman like grizzly bear. We not know what they do. We are afraid such person. Maybe they kill somebody.

"My father say, long time ago when Inuit did not like such person, people say such person must die. They pick someone to kill him — maybe shoot or strangle him. We used to think long time ago, that people when they were — " the old man hesitated.

"Violent?" John asked.

"Yes, violent. Violent people or ones with mind

not right must die.   That was long time ago."

"That was capital punishment!" Paul exclaimed.

"Long time ago, before Inuit live by white man's law, families have to make own laws.   My father says he know one — what you say — violent man that was killed by own son.   Family was better then."

"Did they sometimes kill women?" Paul asked.

Grandfather stared at the waving fireweed in the yard.   "My father say he remember one woman was witch.   People know bad spirits are in her.   She blow breath at people.   She put them under spell. People at settlement are afraid.   They say she must die.   Woman's son and another man kill her."

"That's terrible, Grandfather," John said.

The old man nodded.   "Better now."

John continued.   "Now she would go to a doctor, maybe they'd fly her to Inuvik or Yellowknife, or somewhere for help."

"It must be better for your people now," Paul said, his eyes on Grandmother's broad back as she washed dishes.

"Sometime good, sometime bad," Grandfather said. "Now Inuit get government money.   It make some people lazy.   They don't hunt or trap.   They wait for check, then get drunk.   Not good."

"We have people like that in the United States, too."

"Your people same like Inuit?"

"Some.   But more are like you and Grandfather Nigiyak and your children.   All of you have worked

176

for your living."

Grandfather nodded his agreement.   In a moment he went on. "When I was boy we have good times — not all bad.   Winter time when there was food, inside house we tell stories, do string games and we wrestle, have tug-of-war or drum dance outside when weather is good. Many good times."

Paul stared outside at the cloudless sky.   "I want to always remember how it is here in the Arctic."

They sat, each with his own thoughts, for a long time.

6

SURVIVAL

The distant sound of a plane motor broke the stillness of the afternoon air. Paul and John stopped playing catch to listen.

Paul shouted, "Maybe it's Walter! Let's go!"

They sprinted the short distance to the water's edge and arrived as Walter's orange and black four passenger single Cessna landed on the dusty runway. A passenger followed the pilot from the little plane.

"Hi!" both young men shouted.

"Hi, fellows. This is Jim Arnold. He is the new manager of the Hudson's Bay Company store." Walter pulled a suitcase from the plane. "I'll see you when I'm in Aklavik, Jim," he said.

"Sure," the young man replied taking his luggage and starting toward the store.

"What are you fellows doing here?" Walter asked.

"Haven't you been in Tuk lately?" John said. "We thought our fathers would have told you we were here and that we wanted you to fly us home."

"It's been three weeks since I was in Tuk."

John explained, then he said, "We don't have much money but our fathers will pay you."

"Sure," Walter agreed. "I don't have other passengers out of here. We can start as soon as I've gassed up and you are ready."

They hurried to Grandfather Katoayak's place to get their few possessions. Grandmother bustled around the kitchen as Grandfather talked. "John, tell father he should come see us in winter."

"I'll tell him." John rolled his clothing inside his sleeping bag.

Grandfather reached under the bed and pulled out a fishing rod. "You can have, John. I win in contest at store."

"Thanks, Grandfather. It's nice."

Grandmother shuffled in with a roll of fur in her arms. She spoke to Grandfather. "She say," he interpreted, "she want John take grizzly bear rug to mother."

"Wow! That's a beauty!" Paul exclaimed.

"My mother will like it," John said.

Grandmother smiled and stooped to pull a cardboard box from under the bed. She took out two pair of sealskin moccasins.   One pair she gave to John and the other to Paul.

"For me?" Paul asked.

Grandmother nodded.   John already had his shoes off and was trying on the moccasins.   "They're the right size."   He said something in Inutitut to his grandmother.

Grandfather said, "She make things in winter."

Paul walked back and forth in the new moccasins. "I'll wear them every evening in the dorm.   Will you tell her I like them?"

John repeated the message to his grandmother. When she smiled the laugh lines around her eyes and mouth grew very deep.

Grandfather spoke to the old woman.   She shuffled out to the kitchen and squatting, she pulled out a five gallon can from a low cupboard.

"Muktuk?" John asked.

The old lady nodded.   Grandfather explained, "It's for all of family."   He spoke to his wife again who went to the cupboard and returned with a cardboard box which she gave to John.   "Mipku," she said.

"So many gifts, it's like Christmas," John said.

Grandfather limped over to pick up the can of muktuk and Grandmother shuffled behind helping the boys carry things to the plane.

"We will miss you," the old man said.   "Nice when you are here, like when our boys was young."

Paul said, "I've liked being at your place.

180

LURE OF THE ARCTIC

Thanks for having me. Tell Grandmother for me."

Walter stood beside his plane talking in Inutitut to an elderly Eskimo. The teenage boys and young men who had played baseball with Paul and John were standing along the gravel strip to watch them take off. Walter tossed the small bags of clothes and the sleeping bags inside on top of the muktuk and mipku. "Let's go," he said.

Goodbyes were said, the motor started with a roar, and a moment later they were waving to their Aklavik friends as the little plane rolled down the dusty runway. Then they were airborne and headed northeast toward Tuktoyaktuk.

A haze lay over the delta. Paul stared down at the water intermeshed with land and thought it was difficult to know whether they were flying over water filled with hundreds of islands or tundra invaded by numerous channels, ponds and lakes. With the Peel Channel and Aklavik behind them, there was no sign of life. The colors of spruce, poplars and willows mingled with the light green of grass near the water's edge and the brownish green of tundra grass on the large islands. "It's a tundra tapestry," he thought. He smiled as he remembered Miss Barnes, his second year English instructor. She'd approve of his description of the delta.

Shortly after take-off wisps of ground fog floated over the delta like a gauzy veil. "Pretty, huh?" John shouted. "I've never been up before."

Paul nodded. He nudged John and pointed to an

oil well which showed through a break in the ground fog. Then suddenly it was as though the earth was covered with a downy white blanket. No longer could they see land or water.

"Looks like snow!" John yelled.

"Yeah," Paul answered under his breath.

The sun shone in the window from the southwest but now and then the plane flew through wisps of fog at their level. Walter turned to John. "Like flying?"

"Yeah. Only I'd rather see the ground."

"We'll fly out of this," Walter shouted. But he was wrong, for soon they entered fog so thick that not a glimmer of sun could be seen. Two or three minutes later Walter reached for his headphones and turned on the radio.

"This is Cessna C GPTM calling Inuvik. Fogged in. Approximately twenty-five miles northwest of Inuvik. Supply help or directions. Come in Inuvik." He waited, then tried again.

"Cessna C GPTM calling Inuvik. Approximately twenty-five miles northwest of Inuvik at two thousand feet. Inbound to Inuvik. Supply directions," Walter called. Again he waited, then tried again — and again — and again.

The words, "Fogged in. Supply directions," kept pounding in Paul's mind. Over and over he heard them. He tried to see the sun. Which direction should it be? He looked over his right shoulder toward what he thought was the direction of Aklavik.

Not a glimmer. Drops of moisture were forming on the plane window and skittering backward.

"We're in trouble!" John shouted.

Paul nodded. Walter still was trying the radio. "Cessna C GPTM — Inuvik — need directions —" Paul thought Walter must have decided to go to Inuvik because it was nearer than Tuk and also because the tower was better equipped than the airport at Tuk. "Come in Inuvik. Fogged in —" On and on the call for help continued but no answer came.

Carl. He'd say Walter was shiftless. The radio hadn't worked weeks before when Paul and his father had flown with Walter to Tuk. Why hadn't he had it repaired? "Come in Inuvik — need directions —"

Even if they were directly over the airport they couldn't get down to the runway in the dense fog without direction from the tower.

Walter took off the earphones. "We'll go back to Aklavik!" he shouted. He watched the instruments as the plane banked and leveled. Paul glanced at his watch in the dim light. They should be back in twenty minutes, he estimated. By six o'clock they should be in Aklavik.

The little plane flew on but the fog remained as thick as when they changed directions. There had been no fog when they left. Was it possible that the settlement now was completely fogged in? They'd been gone less than half an hour. Paul held his watch close to his eyes. Twenty-five minutes since they'd turned back.

Walter took the plane down.   "Maybe we'll find a hole."

They watched and hoped for a break in the fog. They waited.   Two — three — five minutes.   Nothing. Not a glimpse of water or tundra below.   Not a bright spot that would show where the sun was.   And Aklavik — where was it?   Maybe they had already passed over the settlement — or maybe they were nowhere near it.   What if the whole delta was blanketed with this thick murky cloud?

Paul tried to put worrisome thoughts from his mind.   In the semi-darkness of the plane he glanced at John's face.   His dark skin seemed more pale than usual.   Perhaps it was the poor light.   John met his gaze.

"Walter's a good pilot," he said.   "He'll find a way."

"Sure."   Paul tightened his seat belt.

The plane banked sharply to the left.   When it leveled Walter shouted, "We'll try going south. Maybe we can get down at Fort McPherson or Arctic Red River."

"How far are those places?" Paul called to John.

"Maybe ninety or a hundred miles."

Water was making zig-zag rivulets across the plane windows.   If they didn't find a hole in the fog at Fort McPherson or Arctic Red River, how long could they fly before they ran out of gas?   A sudden chilling thought struck Paul's mind.   Suppose Walter had not filled the gas tank at Aklavik but had only put in enough fuel to carry them to Tuk?   If that was the case they wouldn't have enough gas.   They must already have flown more than a hundred miles. He could ask Walter but he hesitated, fearful of what the answer might be.

Minutes passed.   The plane droned on.   They'd get out of this somehow.   Walter had flown for several years.   He must have been in dangerous situations before, probably he'd been in dense fog and found his way down.

John's voice roused Paul.   "Walter!   Do we have gas to get to Fort McPherson or Arctic Red River?"

The pilot ran his hand through the long black hair that hung over the collar of his plaid jacket. "It will be close," Walter answered over his shoulder.   Immediately he turned back to watch the instruments.

All the hope Paul had built up disappeared.   They would run out of gas and crash miles from anywhere. And if they didn't, what chance did they have of finding a tiny settlement in the fog in this vast Arctic northland?   He recalled newspaper stories of people who had crashed in the far North.   Some of them never had been found.   Others had been rescued nearly starved and with frozen hands and feet after days of being lost.   But this was summer.   They wouldn't freeze.   What would happen to them?   Maybe — "Hey!"   There's the sun!" he shouted as they broke out of the fog into bright sunlight.   But below, the earth still was blanketed with heavy white mist.

John was smiling now. "We're headed south. Walter knows what he's doing!"

The pilot silently studied the instruments. "Look!" Paul yelled. "There's a break! There are trees and water!" Five minutes later every trace of fog had disappeared.

"Gas's about gone!" Walter yelled. "Be sure your belts are tight. If we have to land, put your head between your knees." He turned back to scan the earth below.

There was a river down there. Not big enough for the Mackenzie. They had left the lake and pond infested delta behind. At least they would crash on solid land. They waited, every muscle tense. A few minutes later the motor coughed, sputtered and died. There was a level spot ahead to the right.

"We're going down!" Walter shouted turning off the ignition. His voice was loud in the suddenly quiet interior of the plane. Paul put his head down and waited. The swish of the air as it flowed past the Cessna sounded soft and gentle. They were gliding — gliding — gliding — gliding — gliding. How long would it be? A bump of the wheels immediately followed by a crash drove his head into the seat in front of him. Loose baggage flew through the cabin between the seats. The plane was standing on its nose with the tail high in the air.

"Are you all right?" Paul shouted to John.

"Yeah. But Walter is hurt." He worked with the seat buckle.

"Press in the middle of the buckle," Paul said. His belt opened and he fell into the back of the seat before him.   He groped his way to Walter who lay face down over the cowling.

"Is he dead?" John asked fearfully.

Paul lifted a limp right hand and felt the pulse. There it was, rapid but weak.   Thump — thump — thump.   "His heart is beating."

"Geez!" John exclaimed.   "There's blood running onto his pants!"

Paul squatted on a roll of clothing and sleeping bag to look up into the shattered windshield at the still face of the Eskimo pilot.   "His head is bleed-ing.   We've got to lie him down."

John slowly made his way to the plane door on the right side.   After working at it a minute he said, "It's jammed.   Let's try the one on the left side."

Paul slammed his shoulder against the door while John held the latch open.   The little plane rocked. At last he said, "It's no use.   They're both jammed. We'll have to try something else."

They searched in the bottom among the clutter of jumbled objects.   "Here's an axe!" John exclaimed as he unfastened the strap which held the tool.   "I'll try to knock one of the doors open."   He swung the axe against the jammed opening until the power of the blows shook the plane.

Paul searched again and found Walter's pulse as he watched blood drip onto the pilot's soiled jeans. Suddenly the door flew open and a blast of cool air rushed into the cabin. John bent to look outside.

Paul stared thoughtfully at Walter. "I don't think we should move him," he said. "Let's get the luggage out of the way so we can lie him down across the front of the plane. I'll unfasten his seat belt and you ease him down."

Together they lowered Walter to the slanting floor. He moaned and his face twisted as consciousness returned. Dark bewildered eyes stared up at the men through streaks of blood from a scalp wound.

"We crashed," John explained. "Remember?"

Paul lifted Walter's head and pushed the corner of his sleeping bag beneath it. "You were knocked out," he explained silently wishing they had water to clean the nasty head wound. He looked into Walter's eyes. The pupils were strange — one was larger than the other. Without saying a word Walter again lapsed into unconsciousness.

"He's hurt bad," John said.

"Yeah. The bleeding has almost stopped but he might be hurt somewhere else."

"The river should be near those trees," John said motioning to the right. "I'll take the basin from the survival kit and get some water."

"I hope there's one in there," Paul said as he watched John open a box marked "SURVIVAL."

"There is," John said taking a basin and crawling from the awkwardly tilted plane.

Paul spread Grandmother's grizzly bear rug over the unconscious pilot and closed the door. Already the chilly air of the Arctic evening was penetrating the thin walls of the fuselage. He pulled things from the survival box. A three pound can filled with a meal-like substance, a box of matches wrapped in plastic, a hunting knife in a sheath, a spool of fishing line and a package of fish hooks and some clothesline rope. In a small metal box there was a roll of bandage and a few handkerchief-size squares of white cloth.

Walter's breathing was fast, but regular. Maybe he'd be better when he woke up. Opening the plane door, Paul crawled outside. He shivered and absently pulled up the hood of his parka. The ground underfoot was soft and spongy. It was no wonder the plane had nosed over. He leaned against the wing strut wondering what they should do.

"Lost in the Arctic," he said aloud. Wisps of fog were moving in from the direction of the river. Where was Arctic Red River or Fort McPherson? He didn't know which place Walter had been trying to reach. He walked away from the plane, stumbling in the muskeg and thinking the little plane couldn't fly out of the place even if they had gas. A few yards away he turned to look back. The fuselage stood tilted at a crazy angle and the bent and twisted propeller was buried in the soft muskeg.

In the distance a wolf howled. Paul shivered. Would they be found? They had little in the way of supplies and winter was not many weeks away. And Walter — suppose he didn't get better? How long

could they survive in the Arctic? He had never before known such loneliness.

Carl had been right in not wanting him to go on this trip. He'd said something might happen. The fog was moving in fast. He wished John would come back. The wolf howled again. His watch said eight-thirty. He'd read stories about wolves. Would they attack a human? And grizzly bears! There were lots of them in the area south of Aklavik. The only weapons they had were the axe and knife. He took a deep breath, trying to quiet the panic he felt rising within him.

"Do something!" he commanded himself. "Keep busy!"

Trying to run, he stumbled back to the plane and crawled inside. Walter, his face and clothes gruesome with caked blood, was sitting up holding his head.

"You're better!" Paul exclaimed.

"I'm dizzy and sick." He retched, throwing up the remains of his last meal.

"Lie down," Paul said helping the injured man and pulling the grizzly rug over him. Walter choked and tried to sit up.

"Lie down and turn your head if you have to vomit," Paul ordered firmly.

"I see two of you," Walter said weakly.

"You hit your head when we crashed. Lie still and rest." Paul wondered about Walter's eyes. The unnatural-looking pupils were a symptom of concussion he recalled. Almost immediately Walter again lapsed into unconsciousness. The plane smelled of vomit. Paul turned his head and breathed in the crisp air.

"Hey!" he yelled as he ran to meet John who cautiously carried the water-filled basin. "I thought you'd never get back. Walter talked a little, but he's unconscious again."

John didn't say much. He concentrated on carefully placing his feet before moving slowly over the bogs. Finally he said, "I don't know what river this is. It's not the Mackenzie. It's not wide enough. Maybe it's the Arctic Red or the Peel."

Paul stumbled. "Is that good or bad?"

"We'd have a better chance of being found on the Mackenzie."

When they reached the plane John carefully deposited the water on a level spot between two bogs. "Fog's moving in fast," he said. "Can't get more water until it lifts."

Inside the plane Walter slept on. Paul checked his pulse. It was the same, rapid but weak. The stench of vomit filled the cabin. Facing one another they wedged themselves between the plane seats on the floor. For a long time they sat, each one with his own thoughts.

Finally John started toward the front of the plane, holding to the seats so he wouldn't fall on Walter. He rustled around among the sleeping bags and boxes. "We'll have some of Grandmother's mipku for supper." He took a strip of dried whale meat from the cardboard box.

"There's a knife in the survival box," Paul said.

"Good. We should only eat a little of our food. We have to make it last." He hacked the mipku into two small pieces and gave one to Paul.

"Sure is hard to chew," Paul commented. "Great-grandfather couldn't eat it."

John smiled faintly. "Old people without teeth soak mipku in whale oil, or else they cook it."

They were silent as they gnawed on the mipku. Finally Paul said, "Let's try to pull the tail of the plane down so it's level. It would be more comfortable."

They tugged at the tail of the fuselage until the nose of the plane was freed from the soft boggy soil of the tundra. Then they lowered it to the ground.

After drinking a large quantity of water they were ready to try to sleep. They pulled the bear rug high over Walter's shoulders before they each settled into a seat inside their sleeping bags. Warm and comfortable, they talked.

"I hope Walter's better in the morning," Paul worried.

"Why is he unconscious so long?"

"Maybe he has a concussion."

Early the next morning Paul hurried to Walter who was tossing restlessly. "Feeling better?" he asked.

"I'm dizzy and my head aches."

"When the fog lifts so we can get water, you can wash up. You're a mess."

"I guess so. I smell bad. I can smell myself."

While they ate a small piece of mipku and drank water, they talked. Walter said slowly, "I'm not thinking right. Why are we in the plane?"

They explained what happened. Dazedly Walter said, "I don't remember anything after we left Aklavik."

"We have to decide what we're going to do," Paul said. Walter was incapable of making decisions.

"Should we stay here near the plane?"

Walter turned over and slept again. John stared at him and shook his head. "There's no use trying to walk out. We don't know which way to go to Arctic Red River or Fort McPherson. Maybe they're nowhere near here, and there aren't any settlements south of them for a long ways." He shrugged. "Maybe we're already south of them."

"Yeah. I think we should stay here."

"I think so, too," John agreed.

Paul hesitated, almost afraid to ask. "I wonder how often planes fly over here?"

John shrugged. "I don't know."

"Are there fish in the river?"

"I saw some jumping last night. We have fishing tackle. A net would be better, but — " John was silent for a time, then he said, "There's lots of driftwood along the river. As soon as the fog lifts we can gather wood and pile it so that we can make a fire fast if we hear a plane."

"A signal! That's a great idea!" Paul suddenly fell silent, then continued in a quiet tone of voice. "A pilot might think we were camping."

"Once I read about a man who was lost. He built three signal fires in a row along a river. He was rescued because three fires together are an international distress call that pilots everywhere know."

"Wow! That's cool!" Paul studied the dense fog outside the plane window. "No one knows we're missing, so they won't be looking for us," he said

slowly. "Your parents and my father don't know we've left Aklavik. Grandfather Katoayak thinks we're back at Tuk. And Walter — we don't know if he had plans anyone knew about."

"I thought of that."

After a time Paul said, "There's a can of some kind of meal in the survival box. I don't know what it is."

"Yay!" John exclaimed when he saw the coarse meal. "That's pinole! It's ground corn and sugar and it is good energy food. We have muktuk, mipku and pinole and we can catch fish to cook. We won't starve."

"Man, we'll live it up," Paul grinned. But in the back of his mind was the awful fear that they wouldn't be found before winter struck the Arctic with all its fury.

"We'll ration the food, the pinole, mipku and muktuk, and use it only when we can't catch fish or snare small animals," John planned.

"Yeah. We'll save it for an emergency," Paul said slowly.

By noon the fog had lifted. Unable to rouse Walter, they took the water basin and reluctantly left him as they went to explore the river bank.

Small plants, moss and lichens were scattered over the muskeg and beneath the stunted willows, birches and conifers that bordered the river. A stiff breeze blew from the north drying the moisture left by the fog. A swan honked in the distance and a fox eyed the men suspiciously from behind a pile of driftwood that had been carried and deposited fifty feet from the river at high water time.

The young men set out three fish lines, fastening them to large pieces of driftwood. The hooks were baited with pieces of mipku. Exploring along the shore they found a muskrat colony of five houses. Nearby bushes covered with the orange-colored akpik berries provided them with a satisfying snack and drinking from the clear cold river quenched their thirst.

"Where should we put the piles of driftwood for signal fires?" Paul asked.

LURE OF THE ARCTIC

"We have to be close to the signals so we can light them fast when we hear a plane," John said. "But the driftwood is near the river and our plane is half a mile away."

"Yeah."

"We could build a shelter in the edge of the trees near the river and move our things there."

"Do you know how to build a shelter?" Paul asked.

"I read about making a lean-to in a survival book at school."

"Maybe by the time we get it done Walter will be able to walk that far," Paul said hopefully.

"Maybe." John studied the trees and the scattered driftwood. "We could build the lean-to close to that big pile of driftwood. We'll chop down some spruce trees for fresh boughs to cover the roof. Then a fire in front of the open side can keep it warm inside." He dipped the water pan into the water.

"Sounds good."

"I'll take water back and see how Walter is." John started through the trees toward the Cessna.

Paul said, "After I check the lines for fish I'll pick some berries for Walter. See you in a few minutes." He started upstream.

They had a fish! Slowly Paul pulled the silver-colored fish on shore. Elated, he ran several feet from the water before taking the hook from the mouth of the wildly flapping whitefish.

"Man! Fish will taste good!" he said aloud,

planning to barbeque it over an open fire. He put the catch behind a pile of driftwood and hurried upstream to pick berries. When he returned a few minutes later, the fish was gone. He thought perhaps it had flopped behind one of the pieces of driftwood, but though he searched, it was not there.

Suddenly a chill ran up his back as he stared down at huge animal tracks in the damp soil near the river. He shivered. There were more of the same kind of tracks but they were smaller. Only one kind of animal could make tracks like that — a grizzly bear and her cubs.

Glancing toward the spruce trees that lined the river he knew the animals were somewhere nearby, perhaps over there among the trees and brush. Cautiously he started through the stunted evergreens toward the plane, his heart pounding in his ears. Though he tried to walk quietly, his boots crunched through spruce needles and dry cones. Looking over his shoulder his eyes caught a quick movement behind a scraggly pine. Curious, an Arctic fox stepped into the opening and stared at him. Walking cautiously, his eyes constantly scanning the bush, he came at last to the muskeg clearing.

Still holding the berries in his cupped hands, Paul struggled to keep his balance as he hurried toward the plane. The door was open. "John!" he shouted.

His friend reached out to take the berries so he

could climb inside. Walter was washing his hands and face and attempting to clean some of the dried blood and soiled spots from his parka. "You're better," Paul said.

Walter nodded, still scrubbing his jacket. John held out the berries to the injured man. "Can you eat these?"

"Akpiks. Thanks. I'm hungry."

"He can walk," John reported. "He was outside looking at the plane when I got back."

Walter pushed back his long black hair that was matted with dried blood and vomit. "How far is the river?"

"Not far," Paul said. "It's on the other side of the trees."

"I want to clean up and wash my hair as soon as my head stops spinning."

As they washed down a few spoonfuls of pinole with water, Paul told of the huge tracks he had seen. "Whatever it was, it took our fish." He concluded slowly, "I think it was a grizzly bear and her cubs."

"That's all we need," John said. They were quiet for a long time. Finally he made his way to the door carrying the axe and roll of clothesline. "I'm going to set some snares. I saw trails near the muskrat colony. Bring the knife, Paul."

Walter again was lying down. "I'll help tomorrow," he said closing his eyes.

Outside John said, "He's not like himself. I

don't believe he realizes what a spot we're in. And those grizzlies! We have to watch to be sure we don't get between the mother and cubs. That makes a sow fighting mad."

Paul kicked a bog. "We don't have any weapons if she attacks."

"We have the axe and knife."

Entering the bush, they watched for any movement. An Arctic ground squirrel, fat and sleek, gave a warning cry to his neighbors. The call was taken up by others in the colony and as they came closer the cries became loud rich screams.

"Sik-sik," John said. "We'll set some snares

here."

On the sandy ridge near the edge of the trees they set several leaning pole snares. As they worked John explained that when the sik-sik tried to get into his burrow he would be snared by the sliding noose in the end of the piece of clothesline.

Near the fishing lines Paul pointed out the grizzly tracks. Keeping an eye on the trees nearby they hastily checked the lines for fish, but the hooks were empty. Hiking along the edge of the river they watched for more signs of the grizzlies.

John said, "There are fish and berries and lots of sik-sik here. The bears are eating and getting fat so they'll be ready for winter."

"Maybe they'll leave because we're here," Paul said hopefully.

John didn't answer. Near the muskrat houses there were paths which the animals had made through the swampy grass. They set snares in several places.

"If we're lucky we may have a good meal," Paul said. "I'm hungry. That pinole might keep us alive, but I feel as though I haven't eaten in a week."

"We'll catch something," John said confidently.

Back near the fishing lines they began setting up piles of driftwood which would be used for signals. They placed dry grass and fine twigs with splintered kindling in the center and piled larger sticks around the kindling in teepee fashion. Green spruce boughs and moss covered the entire pile of wood.

"That's neat!" Paul exclaimed as he stood back to admire their work.

When they were finished three piles of wood one hundred feet apart along the river bank stood ready to signal their distress to passing aircraft.

John took matches from his pocket. "We should both carry matches," he said giving a cardboard folder to Paul. "Take good care of them," he warned. "There aren't too many folders in the survival kit. The first one to get here when we hear a plane will get the fires going."

"Okay." Paul hesitated. "I wish someone knew we were missing."

"Yeah."

Paul picked up the knife he'd used to shave kindling for the signals and put it in the sheath on his belt. "Better take good care of the knife and axe," he said as though he was thinking aloud. John took the axe and they went again to check the fishing lines.

"We got one!" Paul shouted. Together they pulled in the medium-sized whitefish. John seized it as soon as it was on shore and expertly rapped it on the head, killing it instantly.

"Start a small fire while I'm cleaning it," he ordered. "We'll soon eat!"

Paul hustled and by the time the fish was cleaned and washed the fire was snapping.

John spiked half of a fillet on two green spruce

sticks. Holding the fish over the fire, he turned it often until it was thoroughly cooked. Then, sitting with their backs to the fire, they feasted, finishing the meal with a long drink from the river.

Paul cooked a large piece of fish for Walter while John rebaited the three hooks with pieces of the fresh fish. Silently they made their way through the trees on the way back to the plane. Paul wondered what they would do if they came face to face with the grizzly and her cubs. What could they do against such odds?

As though he knew what Paul was thinking, John said, "Grizzlies are mean, but I don't think she'll bother us if we don't get between her and the cubs."

Walter roused himself to eat the fish and drink some water. Then because the boys insisted, he went outside and walked a short distance. "You have to exercise," Paul said. "You'll get weak staying in the plane all the time." Walter stumbled. "Tomorrow we're going to make a shelter by the river."

The man gave no indication that he heard or understood. They turned back toward the plane. John laughed. "Your plane looked pretty crazy before we straightened it. Its nose was buried in the muskeg and its tail was in the air."

Walter did not answer or look at the plane which had been so important in his life. The two friends exchanged glances.

"Walter, does your head hurt?" Paul asked.

"Huh?" His eyes were blank. He shivered. John

said something to him in Inutitut. Walter nodded.

"Let's get him inside," John said. "He's cold and too sick to be out here."

Later when Walter again was asleep beneath the grizzly rug, the young men went outside. Paul pulled his hood up and stuffed his hands into his pockets. "He's not much better," he said.

"Maybe it will take a few days."

Again, as on the previous evening, the full-throated vibrant cry of a wolf drifted across the half darkness of the tundra. Soon it was joined by other harmonious wolf voices. A tingle ran up Paul's back as the wolf pack howled in chorus for three or four minutes. "Do they know we're here?" he asked.

"They know," John said quietly. When the wolf chorus was over he said, "Tomorrow we will build the shelter. It will be better when we are close to our signals."

"Suppose we hear a plane at night?"

"We'd light the signals. Three fires in a row, or in a group, are a call for help anytime."

Silently they leaned against the wing strut of the plane, each one deep in thought. Suddenly Paul had the feeling that he was being watched. He glanced at the door of the plane. Walter wasn't there. Turning, his breath caught in his throat, for not twenty yards behind were two wolves watching them curiously. "John," he whispered. "Look." He pointed to the wolves.

LURE OF THE ARCTIC

The animals appeared relaxed and comfortable as if they had been sitting there for some time. They gazed at the men as if they were trying to decide what the humans were about.

"Scram!" John shouted waving his arms and jumping at the gray and white animals.

Startled, the wolves sprang to their feet, glanced at one another and then trotted off and disappeared in the semi-darkness. They did not look back.

"Wow!" Paul said. "They were sitting almost within jumping distance of our backs!"

"They are curious but they won't attack us."

"They kill caribou."

"Only sick, old or young ones."

"But I've read stories about wolves attacking humans."

John stirred uneasily. "Maybe it could happen if they were hungry and a person was sick and didn't protect himself."

"Like Walter?"

John didn't answer. The evening air was crisp with a hint of approaching winter. As they climbed into their sleeping bags inside the plane Paul wondered again how long they could survive in winter weather. Fear was constantly at the back of his mind.

When they awoke next morning, blue-black clouds were scudding across the sky driven by a stiff north wind. The gloomy day did nothing to lift their

depressed feelings.

When they checked their snares they found two fat ground squirrels. Quickly John skinned and cleaned them as Paul started a fire. Paul piled driftwood nearby. "Let's keep the fire going as much as we can to save matches," he said.

"When the shelter is done we can keep it going all night, unless it rains or snows," John replied spiking the dressed squirrels on green sticks over the hot fire.

After selecting a site for the shelter between two spruce trees about nine feet apart, Paul searched for straight poles which might be used as a framework for their lean-to, while John chopped the lower branches from two trees. Occasionally they turned the roasting ground squirrels which were gradually becoming an appetizing brown.

After a satisfying meal John took meat and water to Walter while Paul continued gathering wood to build the shelter. When he found two fish on the line he cleaned and filleted them and placed them in a rounded piece of spruce bark to be ready for the next meal. At least, we won't starve, he thought.

When John returned with the clothesline they lashed a ten foot pole between the two spruces about five feet above the ground. "We'll build a framework from the driftwood and cover it with evergreen branches," he explained as he lashed several poles from the ground to the crossbeam.

When the framework was completed spruce branches were placed on the forty-five degree lean-to in the same way shingles are put on a roof, the first row at the bottom and the last row at the top. The brush ends of the branches were placed down, overlapping the butt ends of the previous row.

"Rain runs off better if the branches are put on with the brush ends down," John explained.

At last the entire roof was covered with branches to a depth of six inches. It took another hour of work chopping branches to fill in the triangular sides of their shelter with boughs set butt end up, and the lean-to was completed.

"We'll sleep in it tonight," John said standing

back to admire their day's work.

Paul threw more wood on the fire. "I'm going downstream to pick berries." He took a curved piece of bark which would serve as a container.

"While you're gone I'll check the muskrat snares," John replied as he studied the blue-black clouds to the north.

Tired and hungry Paul made his way downstream. The orange-colored berries, dead ripe in the late Arctic summer, would not hang on the bushes much longer. They must pick as many as they could. He munched on a handful of rose hips. John had said they were good to eat because they contained vitamin C. He supposed that ground squirrels hibernated when the weather became cold. That would be the loss of another kind of food. He studied the steel-gray sky below the dark rolling clouds. "At home we'd say those clouds look like snow," he said aloud.

A movement to the left caught his attention. Turning, he saw two grizzly cubs wrestling beside the river. They were so intent on their play that they had not seen him. A whoofing sound from the right gave warning of danger. Whirling, Paul saw an enormous grizzly whose color varied from gold to deepest chestnut. Each hair of the dark cape over her shoulders was tipped with silver. She reared on her hind legs, snorting and gnashing her teeth before she lumbered along in Paul's direction.

Frozen in his tracks, he watched in horror as the

huge snarling whoofing beast bore down on him. Stepping forward he waved both arms in the air and shouted at the top of his voice, a piercing blood-curdling yell.

The grizzly skidded to a halt barely fifty feet from him, whirled and ran crashing through the berry brush, her cubs close at her heels. She stopped and Paul thought she would charge again. But she turned to the cubs, grumbling and scolding as she lumbered to the northeast with her cubs close behind.

Paul watched until she disappeared over a rise in the tundra. Keeping an eye to the northeast he rapidly stripped berries from the bushes. His heart still pounded wildly. He turned at a shout.

"What happened?" John called. "I heard you yell."

Paul told of his frightening experience ending with the statement, "But I've learned something. Grizzlies can be chased away."

"Sometimes. They have a mean disposition. You were lucky."

The wind pushed hard against them. "It will be good to stretch out in our shelter tonight," Paul said.

John didn't answer. He was searching the sky to the south. Suddenly he broke into a run shouting, "A plane! Hurry!"

Paul dropped the berries as they sprinted toward camp at top speed. But it was a hopeless race. The plane passed overhead before they were more than halfway to the shelter.

"Darn!" Paul panted. "One of us should have stayed there!"

They dropped down by the fire to rest. "Maybe they saw our campfire," Paul said hopefully, "and they'll tell someone we're out here."

John said, "They would think some Inuit were camping on the land. One of us must stay here to light the signal fires when another plane comes."

"Hm-m-m. Maybe they saw the plane," Paul said slowly. He shook his head. "I think they would have circled or they'd have given some sign if they had seen it. They would know a plane wouldn't land out here on the tundra."

"Yeah. They didn't see it."

They sat in silence for a long time. Later they barbequed the fish Paul had cleaned earlier in the day. They planned as they ate. "We caught a muskrat," John said. "I was ready to skin him when you yelled at the bear. The meat is good roasted, and we'll save the hides from the rats and sik-siks we catch to keep the kindling dry at the bottom of the signals."

"I hope we're not going to be here long enough to cover all that dry grass and bark at the bottom of the signals!" Paul retorted.

John went on. "Starting tomorrow we should try to get as many fish, rats, and ground squirrels as we can."

"They'll spoil."

John shook his head. "We'll dry some of the fish and meat and we'll dig a hole down to the permafrost. Meat will keep frozen there until we need it."

"Do ground squirrels hibernate?

John nodded. "That's why we should get as many as we can now."

"I think I could get some by hitting them with rocks."

"Great. We'll need plenty of food if we're not found soon," John said.

Back at the plane Walter seemed more alert. He wondered where John was. As he ate his portion of fish Paul explained that someone must be near the signals.

Walter nodded. "I heard a plane."

"Yeah. It was gone before we got to the signals."

Paul collected their clothing, sleeping bags and the bear rug. "We're going to sleep in the new shelter tonight," he explained.

They climbed from the plane. Though he was unsteady, Walter held to Paul's arm and they slowly made their way across the bogs to the lean-to.

"Welcome to our new home, Walter!" John said.

The pilot dropped to the ground beside the campfire. "My head is dizzy," he said leaning against a tree.

"You can rest now," John said. "I'll go to the plane to get some of our things." He turned to

Paul. "We'd have better beds if the floor was covered with spruce branches."

"Okay. I'll do that while you carry the supplies." He took the axe from the shelter. Walter, his head against the trunk of a tree, was sleeping. The wolves were tuning up for their evening chorus. Paul stood by the fire and listened. He could distinguish individual voices in the chorus as the sounds rose and diminished in intensity. First came a low mournful moan that stirred his emotions and lasted from ten to fifteen seconds, then another voice joined in, then another and another. The music grew in intensity until Paul thought the whole pack must have joined in the evening symphony. Again the mournful harmonious blending of their voices sent a tingle up his back. It reminded him of a feeling he once had at the bowel-shaking throb and thunder of a superb organ played by a master musician in his grandmother's church in Detroit. He was sorry when the wolves' symphony suddenly ended.

Methodically he proceeded chopping branches from the evergreens, and placing them to a depth of six inches on the floor of the six by eight foot lean-to.

With their muktuk, mipku and pinole, the survival box and their sleeping gear and clothing transferred to the shelter, the three friends bedded down. The fire burned cheerfully in front of the opening, casting flickering shadows on the inside of the spruce lined shelter. When Paul or John awoke they placed more wood on the fire. John had said, "It warms the shelter and will keep grizzlies away while we sleep."

Next morning a heavy frost coated the willows beside the river and the russet-brown grass of the tundra. Another short Arctic summer was nearing its end. The gray-green of the tundra plants was changing daily to the gold, maroon and russet-brown of autumn.

The day was a busy one. Walter stayed near the shelter dozing by the fire while John cleaned fish and hung the fillets over a line to dry. Paul checked the snares for game. Dry threads of gray-white lichen snapped underfoot as he walked. The noise alerted an Arctic fox running to her den with a fat ground squirrel dangling from her jaws. As he neared the ground squirrel colony a sharp call of "Sik-sik" warned other squirrels of an intruder. The call was picked up and repeated as the little animals scampered into their burrows with tails flicking. The skittish squirrels were curious for they constantly peeped out of burrows to scream "Sik-sik" before again hiding in their underground tunnels.

Paul removed a small rock from his pocket, took aim and a fat ground squirrel lay stunned on the tundra. "Hm-m-m," he mused as he picked it up. "That was easy."

There were dozens of the little animals. An especially bold one scolded him. Taking three ground squirrels from the snares he quickly killed them with a sharp rap on the head from the handle of the hunting knife. Resetting the snares he started back by way of the muskrat colony where he found a snared rat. Emerging from between dwarfed willows Paul heard splashing water and caught a glimpse of movement in the marshy channels beyond the muskrat colony. He shrank back behind the scraggly brush and parted the slender shoots. A wolf, his grayish-white fur dripping water, waded upstream in one of the larger muskrat channels, splashing noisily as he went. Puzzled, Paul watched as the wolf continued into a progressively narrower and more shallow channel. Finally when the water was only a few inches deep, the wolf dove his nose into the water and with one quick chop of his jaws, he broke the back of a squirming northern pike.

"Wow!" Paul breathed. "He's fishing! I'll bet we could do that if we had a spear."

Back at camp Paul explained what he had seen. John and Walter never had heard of wolves fishing but both agreed they might take a tip from the wolf.

"They're smart," John said. "I've heard Grandfather tell about how they hunt caribou. He says they think almost like we do in hunting."

"I could make a spear," Walter suggested when there was a lull in the conversation, and after you drive the fish down the channel into shallow water, you'd spear it."

"Good idea!" Paul exclaimed, pleased that Walter

was able to help them plan their survival.

"I'm still dizzy," the pilot went on, "but if you'll cut an inch and a half green pole, I'll make you a spear."

John found a green sapling and removed the branches and bark. Walter then split the pole about eighteen inches from the end. With a short length of clothesline he wrapped the pole tightly so it would not split farther. The point was sharpened and notches or teeth were carved in the inside edges of the spear. The tips were gently spread and a thin twig inserted to hold them open.

"The twig is the trigger," Walter explained. "We'll take it out when we don't use the spear so the sides can go together to keep the spring in the wood."

"That's cool," Paul said with admiration.

Walter leaned his head back against a tree. "I used to spear fish when I was a youngster," he said wearily.

John stayed in camp to skin and clean the game while Paul went to try out the spear. Walter removed his high rubber boots. "Use mine," he suggested tossing the boots to Paul. "The water would go over yours."

As he pulled the boots on Paul asked, "How about the wolf? What should I do if he's there?"

"He'll run. He might watch you but he won't attack," John said. Walter nodded.

Hurrying along the river toward the muskrat colony Paul was startled by a pair of whistling swans that took off with a great splashing of water and flapping of wings. The steel gray sky had an unfriendly appearance. There had been no sun for two days. Perhaps a storm was coming.

Arriving near the shallow channel, Paul searched the clear water for fish. He waded near the edge of the river hoping to frighten a pike into the reeds. He splashed up the channel in imitation of the wolf. A muskrat swam ahead of him and disappeared into the willows. Ducks quacked in the distance.

At last, discouraged by his lack of success, Paul returned to camp by way of the berry meadow. Accustomed during his lifetime to a daily diet of fresh fruit and vegetables, his body craved a change from the constant meat and fish diet so satisfying to his Eskimo friends. Keeping a wary eye out for the grizzlies, Paul found the bark container he had discarded when they heard the plane. It was empty. Probably Canada jays or maybe mice or lemmings had eaten the fruit.

Quickly Paul stripped berries from the bushes, eating as he picked. Soon his craving was satisfied and the bark basket was filled.

Back at camp Walter slept inside the shelter and the fat muskrat roasted on a spit over the fire. At one side of the lean-to John dug a hole with a crude shovel he had made from twelve-inch sticks laced flat to the end of a four foot pole. The tip of the shovel had been sharpened so that it worked quite well in the soft soil.

"This hole is our freezer," John said. "I'll go down another foot and I should reach the permafrost."

Paul looked into the eighteen-inch-deep hole. "We should have plastic to keep the meat clean."

"My people have survived because they use what they have. That is what we'll do." John threw out another shovelful of dirt. "We'll use moss and lichens in the bottom and we'll pack the meat and fish in it. Then spruce boughs can go over the top."

John rested on his shovel. "Tomorrow I'll set more snares and fish lines, and maybe we can spear some fish. You'll be able to get more sik-sik with your good pitching arm. We'll pick lots of berries and rose hips. We need as much food as we can get. Soon it will be cold enough to cache meat and fish, and we can leave our food in the freezer until later."

"Cache?" You mean fasten it in a tree?"

"In a tree or from poles. But animals and birds will steal it if they can."

Paul gathered a pile of moss and lichen. At last they were finished. That night as they ate the roasted muskrat and fresh berries and drank the pan of Labrador tea prepared by John, they felt comfortable and satisfied.

"This tea is good," Paul said sipping the fragrant spicy beverage. "How did you make it?"

"I picked the leaves and dried them in a pan over the fire until they were crumbly," John replied, "and then put them in boiling water. I've heard Great-grandfather talk about Labrador tea. Walter showed me what the plant looked like. There's lots of it growing around here."

Walter shifted his position. "Labrador tea also is good if it's made from freshly picked green leaves," he commented. He grinned. "Eskimos have to have their mug-up, Paul."

Tired, fed and relaxed, they crawled inside the warm lean-to. Paul thought before he drifted off to sleep how great this experience would have been if it were just a camping trip. But instead they were lost. Lost on the tundra of the vast Northwest Territories, and no one knew they were missing.

THE RELENTLESS ARCTIC

Two weeks passed. Paul and John hunted and fished to stock their permafrost freezer. Paul's ability as a baseball pitcher enabled him to knock senseless many ground squirrels by a blow to the head with rocks he picked up along the river. They continued to snare rabbits, muskrats, ground squirrels and ptarmigan. A long line of fish fillets hung drying beside the lean-to. They speared a few pike but most of the fish were caught on lines they had set out. Several caches of game wrapped in bark hung on poles near the shelter. Bark baskets contained quarts of berries and rose hips.

Walter, though plagued by headaches, dizziness and partial loss of memory, helped to skin and clean the game. Uppermost in the minds of all three was the certain knowledge that with their meager supply of clothing, supplies and shelter, they could not survive the many months of an Arctic winter. Each one, however, kept his dismal thoughts to himself and pretended cheerfulness, knowing there was a chance the crew of a plane might discover them.

The daylight hours were growing shorter, the nights were cold and the almost constant north wind found its way through the flimsy shelter. In the morning the partially frozen muskeg felt less spongy beneath their feet. Whistling swans and ducks were heading south on their annual migration to warmer climates. The tundra was burnished with autumn colors of brown and red and gold. From a distance patches of waving cotton grass looked like snow. There was a grayness in the air. The blurred sun appeared unfriendly and cold and the steel-gray sky carried a fearful threat of days to come.

Sitting about the fire after a midday meal of boiled fish, the three friends shared scalding Labrador tea from their one cooking utensil. Across the river a wolf hunted on the tundra for mice and lemming as she ignored the watching humans. "It's as though we have an agreement," Paul said. "The wolves know we're here but they ignore us and we don't bother them."

The graceful animal pounced, dove her head into the brown moss and came up with a struggling lemming which she quickly gobbled. Working her way upstream near the river she paused to study a flock of ducks that had interrupted their migration journey to feed. A hundred yards away from the ducks, the wolf began to act as if she had suddenly become demented. Yipping like a puppy, she chased her tail; she rolled over and stopped to lie on her back with all four feet waving furiously in the air.

"She's gone out of her mind," Paul said.

The wolf leaped wildly into the air, snapping at nothing while she uttered shrill squeals. The ducks were hypnotized by curiosity. They swam in for a closer look at the ridiculous-acting animal. Closer and closer they came, their necks outstretched, quacking in wonder among themselves. And the closer they came, the crazier grew the wolf's behavior.

When the leading duck was about ten feet from shore, the wolf gave a mighty leap toward it. There was a great splash, a frenzied whacking of wings, and all the ducks but one were up and away.

Leaping from the near freezing water the wolf killed the duck with a quick bite. She then dried herself with a series of furious shakes which sent a mist of water droplets in all directions. Then, without a backward glance at the camp across the river, she padded across the tundra carrying her catch. Shortly afterward the lone voice of a distant wolf came from the north to be almost immediately answered by an animal nearby.

"The wolves are talking," Walter commented.

LURE OF THE ARCTIC

A lone caribou bull, stately in his fall coat with sleek brown fur down his back and deep underhang of white fur on his chest, trotted toward the south on the opposite side of the river. His face was proud and sullen. A last tatter of velvet hung from the tip of one horn. His antlers were dry but still slightly tinged with blood. He swam the river and disappeared over the tundra.

"The first one," Walter said.

"Why haven't we seen them before?" Paul asked.

"They've been north. Now it is time for the fall migration to the forests where they will stay in winter. Soon now they'll be coming."

"If we only had a rifle," John mused.

Early the following morning a sound came from downstream that caused the men to rush outside, almost falling over one another. Across the river was the spearhead of the fall caribou migration, a column of animals plodding southeastward. The only sound was the characteristic snapping of caribou hooves and the chuh, chuh, chuh of many hooves in the frozen grass, interspersed occasionally by the "Mah!" of a calf.

They watched the ungainly animals move steadily ahead, their heads thrust awkwardly down and forward. Though they appeared clumsy they rapidly moved forward over the half-frozen leathery tundra.

"Tuktu. Many tuktu," John murmured.

The herd was not wandering but going steadily along the river, then crossing upstream where it

curved eastward across their route to the southeast.

"They know," Walter said. "The Arctic night, the hungry time is coming. They are safe in the forests to the south."

Silently John took the hunting knife from his belt. As the others watched the caribou, he bound the handle of the knife to a pole with a piece of clothesline so that the blade protruded its full length from the end. "I'm going to get a caribou," he announced.

223

"It's worth a try," Paul said.

Walter picked up the axe. "Down by the bend in the river there's a place to hide," he said.

Moving cautiously between the scraggly evergreens, they slipped toward the spot where the migrating herd came from the water. Paul followed carrying a strong club. He watched as his friends worked their way closer to the moving animals.

Suddenly Walter and John sprang forward to meet the dripping wet caribou. In terror the animals turned back toward the river but in that split second John and Walter struck. Walter slammed the axe into the head of a large bull, dropping it in its tracks. John had rammed the spear into a fat cow's shoulder. Struggling, she ran pulling John as she desperately tried to get away. Paul struck the weakened cow in the head with his club. Finally she dropped.

The steadily flowing herd now crossed the river a short distance from the original crossing, moving ahead toward their destination to the southeast.

Exhausted, Walter returned to camp while the young men dragged the dead animals to the shelter. Resting by the fire with a pan of steaming Labrador tea, they watched the caribou herd. Some of them had problems. A cow limped. A bull held his mouth open, panting. A cow drew to the side of the column to nurse her calf as the others, the bulls, cows and calves passed her. She pulled herself away from the calf and at once she was trotting. The calf shook his head, then was trotting after his mother. A big bull sped past the calf. He was grayish brown with a silvery belly stripe. His antlers were held high. His body flowed along and Paul sensed his reserve of physical strength.

The line swung past, the light gleaming off their antlers. The only sounds were the chuh, chuh, chuh of large feet and the clicking of hooves.

Paul and John skinned and cut up the two animals. Most of the meat was packed in the permafrost freezer, but some was cut in thin strips to dry. Now and then one of them paused to turn a large piece of a caribou hind leg that roasted over the fire.

"Man! That will taste good!" Paul exclaimed as he sniffed the appetizing odor of roasting meat. "I had caribou steak in Inuvik. I'm glad we have all this meat!"

"Yeah," John agreed. "But it's good we have the hides too. We'll need them to keep warm." He looked into the shelter, "Are you all right, Walter?"

The man raised up on his elbow. "I'm okay. I was dizzy again, but it's better now."

By night a few caribou still passed, their feet making a sound of shuh-wih, shuh-wih, over frozen grass, a gentle sound like that of pouring granulated sugar from one pile to another. By the next day they passed in scattered column formation, but there were longer intervals between bands. These later animals were in poor condition, many with

their ribs showing. Tired limping calves, their heads bobbing up and down. Weary, sick cows. A cow with sharp little antlers slowly made her way along the migration route. She favored a front leg, her head going up and down with each step. Slowly she struggled along unaware of her fate.

"Look," Paul whispered. "Wolves!"

As the limping animal bobbed a few more tortuous steps the pack descended upon her. She was down almost immediately and shortly thereafter the struggle was over.

"Wow!" Paul exclaimed. "They're vicious!"

Walter agreed. "The caribou feeds the wolf, but the wolf keeps the herd strong for he kills the old, the sick and the weak. Old Inuit have always known this was true. White men say wolves should die because they kill too many caribou, but the wolf needs the caribou to live, and the caribou needs the wolf to keep the herd healthy."

"Wolves are not like men," John commented, "For they only kill to eat, not for fun."

Paul mused, "There were a lot of caribou in this herd. Seems as though the Inuit would have all the caribou they need."

"To you it seems there were many. In the old times migrating herds took days to pass. This time there were not many."

After the last of the caribou passed the days were uneventful. By mid-September the tundra plains burned with a subdued glow of russet where frost had touched the low shrubbery. A few days were bright under a clear sun but most were dismal and gray and nights were uncomfortably cold with below freezing temperatures.

"We have been here a month," Paul said checking the notches they carved daily on an evergreen tree which served as their calendar. "My friends are back at college — and my parents and Karen don't know I'm alive. Maybe Dad has left Tuk by now —" his voice trailed off.

"If only a plane would come —" John added.

"The letters on my plane would tell them who we are — if they checked it out — and if they saw it," Walter said softly.

"And if it was daytime, and if they were flying

low enough to see it, and if they were watching. There's too many ifs." Paul's tone was despondent.

"For some reason the plane that went over that evening when we first got here missed seeing it. They surely couldn't miss our signals if they burn good," John said.

Walter mused, "I still can't remember what happened after we left Aklavik. And I don't remember anything that happened for a few days after we crashed."

"Well, you're better now," Paul said. In a moment he added somewhat reluctantly, "Walter, I've wondered why you didn't have your radio repaired. Remember, it didn't work when you flew us from Inuvik to Tuk?"

The pilot shook his head. "I've had problems with it several times. The repairman always thinks it is in perfect condition when he's through tinkering. But this time when it quit, it was serious." He hesitated, then added, "But I still think we'll make it somehow."

For a few minutes John studied the northern sky, which was filled with dark clouds. "What do you think, Walter?" he asked. "Does the sky look like snow?"

"I think so. We're lucky it hasn't come before."

Low dark clouds in the north rolled threateningly. Paul shivered, as much from fear of the future as from the cold. He threw some wood on the fire and ran upstream to gather more driftwood to add to their supply.   There was grayness in the air and the constant whuff of wind around the flimsy shelter.   The tundra seemed dead and empty of life.

John checked the kindling and moss in the center of each signal for dryness, carefully covering it with ground squirrel and muskrat hides. The rest of the day he and Paul gathered and chopped wood in preparation for bad weather. The brown tundra was covered with amber light through which an occasional snowflake drifted. Suddenly the gusts changed to a hard steady wind from the north, and the snowflakes, widely separated, became horizontal streaks.

Inside the shelter away from the wind they were dry and less uncomfortable than in the open. Outside was the amber light over the brown earth, and the winding ice-rimmed river and the empty tundra.

That evening Paul and John stood by the campfire observing a display of Northern Lights. Beautiful oscillating greens shading into pink and red shot upward in beams of color which changed position and brilliance from second to second. The bands of color shifted across the northern sky like pastel curtains of colored light waving in the wind. The flickering frost-white beams and ever changing hues were breathtaking in their beauty.

Finally Paul said softly, "I'll never forget your Arctic sunsets and Northern Lights. We see Northern Lights sometimes at home, but they don't compare to this." He motioned.

John replied, "I never tire of watching them. We learned in school that the displays take place about seventy miles above the earth and that sometimes they're several hundred miles high. The older Inuit have many legends about them."

Paul laughed. "I can see why they would. Though we know the explanation, they still seem almost magical." They hurried inside the shelter.

During the night, snow came. Wind drifts formed behind each shrub. This snow would not melt until spring.

Paul wakened with a start. Something had startled him. He poked his head outside his sleeping bag. In the dim light he saw the fire had gone out. He listened. Something was moving the evergreen branches over the permafrost freezer. He nudged John and Walter. Peering around the side of the shelter, his heart raced.

"Grizzly," he hissed. "Yell!" He grabbed the axe.

Rushing outside, jumping, yelling, screaming and waving their arms while Paul swung the axe about his head, they presented a frightening spectacle to the surprised grizzly. She whirled dropping a piece of caribou meat before she fled whuffing across the tundra. From somewhere nearby her cubs scrambled to join and keep up with their lumbering mother.

"She'll be back," Walter muttered.

"When do bears hibernate?" Paul asked as he in-

spected the huge tracks in the snow and the damage the grizzly had done to their store of meat.

"Soon. It's not cold enough yet."

John came from the opposite side of the shelter. "The cubs tore down two of our caches but part of the meat can be saved. We scared them away just in time."

"The mother is too heavy to climb to the caches, but not the cubs," Walter said as he rearranged and covered the meat in the ground freezer.

Because of the snow the fire was slow to start. After it was blazing and breakfast was roasting, Paul said, "If we hear a plane we're going to have to move fast to light the signals, especially if the wood is covered with snow. Each of us should light a fire."

John agreed. "Walter could do the one closest to the shelter, I'll take the one to the right, and you do the left one. And be sure we always have dry matches in our pockets."

"Yeah, man!" Paul muttered.

That night they slept fitfully. The same thought was in everyone's mind. Suppose the fire went out and the grizzly attacked them in their sleep. Someone was up every hour to pile on more wood. At last, exhausted, they fell into a deep sleep.

Paul and Walter wakened at the same time. John was gone. The fire, though nearly burned out, smoldered on the ends of several long pieces of driftwood. Feeling for the knife in his belt Paul stepped outside into the morning light just as John yelled, "Help!"

Paul was frozen to the spot by the terrifying sight before him. Reared on her hind legs the grizzly was woofing, growling and chopping her jaws. She dropped and charged John with a half growl, half scream of rage, her mouth drooling flecks of foam while she made short grunting sounds. Their supply of meat was scattered for yards around.

Walter and Paul yelled and waved their arms, but the grizzly kept coming. With a terrible roar she charged. Intent on disposing of John, she ignored them. She uttered a low growl and with one swat of her huge paw John flew ten feet against a tree. He was knocked senseless.

The sight of his friend lying unconscious on the ground with the huge brute standing over him spurred Paul to frantic action. The enormous grizzly nudged John's neck. Paul grabbed the knife from his belt and yelling, he ran toward the bear. She reared, then dropped down to stand over John.

With another yell Paul leaped on the grizzly's back. Crazed with desperation and fear he plunged the knife into her shaggy neck fur. Pulling himself higher on the bear's hump he slashed again and again at her neck. As her warm blood spurted the grizzly let out a deafening roar and snapped her head back. The quick action sent the knife flying from Paul's hand.

As he slid down her back the huge beast grabbed him with both paws and crushed him to her chest. She squeezed harder. Bones popped. He felt a stab of pain. The smell of her blood and fur nauseated him.

"This is it," he thought. "There's no use." He stopped struggling. As soon as he was quiet she dropped him and turned to meet Walter who was yelling as he came at her with a blazing pole from the fire. She reared, her mouth open wide. With deadly accuracy Walter charged at the seven hundred pound grizzly to ram the blazing pole down her throat. With a roar of pain and rage she dropped to all fours, shook her great head, whirled and lumbered away at a surprisingly fast speed.

Paul staggered to the fire to arm himself with a blazing torch but the bear, roaring, ambled on out of sight trailed by her frightened cubs.

Their food, the ground squirrels, muskrats, fish, caribou, rabbits, birds, berries and rose hips was trampled and torn into a hodge-podge mess.

Running through what was left of their meager food supply Paul and Walter rushed to help John who was struggling to sit up. A gash gushed blood from his eye to his chin. He shook his head to clear his confused senses.

"Where — where is she?" He appeared dazed as he stared at the blood dripping onto his parka.

"Gone," Paul said holding his side. "But she sure knocked you for a loop."

"It's a wonder she didn't break your neck," Walter said. "They can kill a moose with one swat." He looked at Paul. "Are you all right?"

"I think I have broken ribs."

Walter went to the survival box to get a white cotton square with which he cleaned John's face. "You should have stitches. You'll have a scar," he commented.

John smiled weakly. "Not everyone can boast about a scar made by a grizzly."

"Yeah. My broken ribs don't show." Paul shuddered. "She smelled terrible." He grinned. "Maybe I smelled terrible to her, too. It's been a long time since I've had a good bath."

LURE OF THE ARCTIC

They sat by the fire while Walter fixed Labrador tea. "A mug-up will make us feel better," he said.

For a long time no one mentioned the almost complete destruction of their food supply and the tragic results that could follow. At last Walter said, "I'm going to take a look around."

John removed the wet cloth from his face. "I might as well go help you."

Paul stared into the fire. The destruction of their food was the last blow. Now they didn't have a chance. Painfully he crawled into his sleeping bag and zipped it over his head. He could hear the murmur of John's and Walter's voices. It hurt to breathe. Soon he learned to take very short breaths. He was cold and miserable.

Some time later he unzipped his sleeping bag. He struggled to sit up. The pain in his side was bad. With teeth clenched he finally managed to get to his feet and went to find his friends.

Walter was attempting to salvage their food. Crushed berries and rose hips clung to the few remaining pieces of meat. The snow was stained with berry juice.

"It's garbage," Paul muttered.

Walter looked up. "Thousands of people in the world survive on garbage every day." He packed a piece of berry and pine-needle-covered caribou in the evergreen lined hole in the ground. "We'll get our berries with our meat," he joked. "We'll even have berries with fish." He brushed some dirt from a frozen fillet.

Paul turned away. "Where's John?"

"He's gone to clean the snow off the plane, so the orange and black colors and the letters will show up from the air."

Paul didn't answer. Painfully he walked to the opposite side of the shelter. The two small caches of food on poles and in the tree were undisturned. Apparently the cubs had found enough to do by helping their mother gobble and destroy the food in the freezer. Slowly he made his way back to watch Walter. "You think the grizzly will come back?" he asked.

Walter shrugged. "I don't know. She was hurt and bleeding where you stabbed her, and she must have a sore throat from being rammed with that burning pole." He paused. "Any time now she will go into her den to sleep."

Later that afternoon beside the fire Walter studied the gloomy faces opposite him. "Let's celebrate!" he said suddenly. "John, break open your big can of muktuk."

"Okay. This is as good a time as any, and we do have something to celebrate. At least we're alive, and we have food for a few days."

For the present, Paul thought, but what of the future?

THE END OF AN ADVENTURE

Huddled about the fire Paul and John watched as Walter chipped another niche in the spruce tree. "October first, 1975," he said. "We've been here seven weeks."

"Only one plane in all that time — and we missed it," Paul exclaimed with disgust.

Walter poked the fire savagely. "We have to believe there'll be another. We can't give up. Inuit people have always had to fight to stay alive. We live with one foot in the past and the other in the present, but we will survive."

John gingerly touched the long crust-like scab on his face. "Sure," he said without conviction. Paul stared silently at the barren snow-covered tundra.

237

Walter went to sit inside the shelter on a small log.   He stretched his feet toward the fire.   "Did I ever tell you about my great-grandfather?" he asked.

When his friends did not respond, he continued. "My father's grandfather was Naoyavak.   He died a few years ago."

John muttered, "I never heard of him."

"Once he lived at Kitigazuit west of Tuk."

John nodded.   Walter shoved his hands under his jacket to warm them.   "Sit down, fellows.   I want to tell you about my great-grandfather's life."   When they were settled, their feet extended toward the fire, Walter went on.

"When he was seven years old a bad sickness hit the people at Kitigazuit.   It probably was smallpox. People died like flies.   Only a few families survived.   Though Great-grandfather was small, he remembered two Inuit men spent all their time burying the dead.   They couldn't keep up and finally corpses were left on the ground.   The ones that were living decided to leave Kitigazuit — to get away from the terrible place.

"Among those that died were the parents of little Naoyavak.   He was an orphan, and in those days orphans were almost outcasts."

"Why?" Paul inquired.

Walter rubbed his forehead thoughtfully.   "There was not enough food in winter and parents had a struggle to feed their own children.   After the

remaining people left the area, my great-grandfather, the little Naoyavak, stayed with any family
that would have him. When there was plenty of food,
he ate, but often he was hungry. His clothes were
worn and he was always cold. As he told it he
scrounged for food like a stray dog. Searching,
scavenging, stealing — he did anything he had to
to stay alive.

"The people who were left went to the east and
the summer passed and winter came. One day the
group saw a huge pack of wolves on the ice heading
east. The people said the wolves had eaten the
bodies left at Kitigazuit and that they now were
going on their travels."

Paul shuddered. Walter paused as John poked the
fire and a shower of sparks sailed toward the southeast. "Those days must have been terrible for your
people," Paul said softly.

"But they had good times too. Great-grandfather
told about the way it was inside the igloo. In
those days they had stone lamps called kudlik. They
were made from a block of soft stone."

John said, "I never saw stone like that near
Tuk."

"There isn't any on the Delta of the Mackenzie.
Great-grandfather said they bartered for it with
Inuit to the east, where the bluish-colored stone
was found."

"How did they make lamps?" Paul asked.

"They carved out a long oval shape from the soft

stone. They made wicks from moss or from willow catkins. The women would pound seal fat with a maul and the fat was put at the back of the lamp on the flat section opposite the groove. Then the oil dampened wick was lit and the heat would make the fat melt and drip into the groove, dampening the wick."

Paul said drily, "I'd rather have our electric lights."

"Wouldn't we all?" Walter laughed. "Some of the igloos had lamps three and a half feet long and others had them as long as five feet. The lamps lighted and warmed the igloo."

John said, "Just where was this blue stone found?"

"Eskimos far to the east around Coppermine would trade with ones to the west who needed stone for lamps. The way Great-grandfather told it, they wandered about wherever food was to be found. He said that when they moved the men walked beside the sled, hauling and pushing. Women in front pulled the sled. They wore a sort of harness."

"I thought they used dogs!" Paul exclaimed.

"They did," Walter answered, "but some families had only two dogs and the supplies for a family might weigh two thousand pounds. There were sacks of whale meat, game, fish, skin bags of oil and boards cut from tree trunks they found on the beach.

"When they had food, they stayed inside if the

weather was bad. They told stories, played games and wrestled. They didn't worry much about the future. They knew there would be bad times. That was the way life was."

No one spoke for several minutes. Finally Paul asked, "How did your great-grandfather manage to survive? I'd think he would have died of disease or exposure if he was kicked around from igloo to igloo without warm clothing and with so little food."

"He said he was sick a lot, but no one paid much attention. Probably most of the group hoped he'd die, especially when food was scarce. As I said, they didn't like orphans."

Walter continued. "There was a certain custom among the Inuit at that time. Any person who took part in the hunt would be given a share of the prize. The men didn't want this little kid, my great-grandfather, with them on the hunt, but he'd tag along at a distance. Then when they were successful in getting game, he'd suddenly appear so he could claim his share of the meat. In this way he survived. He said that when he was small he was always afraid.

"Once when he was about ten years old the group was near Coppermine. He said a man from that group was more friendly to him than the others. The man had a son about Great-grandfather's age and they played together. One day the father grabbed Great-grandfather, yanked down his hood and looked at his neck. He was covered with lice. The man took the little orphan to his wife who undressed him and threw away his lice-infested clothes. Then she washed him and gave him some of her son's clothing. The man's name was Atatiak and he belonged to a group of Siberian Eskimos. Great-grandfather lived with them that winter, but he never saw them again after they returned to Russia. He always remembered their kindness."

A sudden blast of wind filled the little shelter with smoke. Coughing and jumping to their feet the men rushed outside for fresh air. They stamped their cold feet and beat their hands together.

Paul muttered, "Wouldn't it be great to sit in a warm room again? But I guess we're lucky if you consider your great-grandfather's young life. Tell us more about him."

They returned to sit on the log inside the shelter and Walter continued. "By the time Naoyavak was fourteen he had learned to snare white foxes. In a year or two he snared enough fur-bearing animals so he bought two dogs and a sled. From then on, life was better for him, especially after he was able to buy a gun, a .44 for which he traded twelve white fox skins. Then he hunted polar bears and seals and snared more white foxes. He made warm clothes for himself from sealskin. Even his boots were made of the sealskin."

John asked, "How did the group treat him after he was able to make his own way?"

Walter smiled. "They accepted him."

LURE OF THE ARCTIC

John commented, "I thought from hearing my great-grandfather's stories that the Inuit people always shared food with other families when food was scarce."

"Families shared, yes," Walter said. "Naoyavak didn't have a family. He was an orphan — an outcast."

"Strange. It was survival of the fittest in those days," Paul commented as he thought what a wealth of information he had obtained about the Eskimos and their ancestors. But right now the chances of his using his knowledge in his social work studies looked pretty slim. He roused himself from his dismal thoughts. Walter was talking.

"Great-grandfather grew up to be a successful hunter." Walter smiled. "I should tell you about the first time he came across the tracks of Nanuk, the great white bear. He was still a boy and he was hunting hare when he saw huge bear tracks, the biggest ones he had ever seen. The heap of dung the bear had left on the snow would have filled a big wash bowl. When he saw it he was so scared that he ran back to camp."

John and Paul laughed. "Guess the bear was big all right," Paul said.

Walter continued. "When Great-grandfather was in his later teens he often traded his animal skins at the Hudson's Bay company at Aklavik. Then he had white man's food — rice, flour for bannocks and sugar. He still moved about a lot. Aklavik, Kitigazuit, Tuk, Hershel — all over the delta area. He also traded with men who were on ships that stopped along the Beaufort shore in summer."

"Sounds as though he had it made," Paul said. "Did he hunt beluga too?"

"He did. That was a very special time. The Inuit considered whale hunting time almost as a celebration." Walter was silent for a time before he said softly, "I wish I had lived in those days."

John said, "You wouldn't have had your plane. I'd rather live now."

Paul asked, "When did Naoyavak marry?"

"About 1915, he thought. My great-grandmother's name was Mary and she was a half breed with French blood. She was a widow with four children. They had several more children, my grandfather Silas, being the oldest."

"Silas Maniksak — I remember him," John said.

"Great-grandfather lived his last years in Coppermine with one of his sons. I only saw him once when I was about twelve, but I never forgot the stories he told."

Silently Paul took the axe and basin and went for water. Reopening a hole in the ice near the edge of the river, he dipped the basin in the icy water. His feet thumped the hard frozen ground. Bending cautiously to protect his healing ribs, he placed the pan over the fire. Being gloomy didn't help their situation. He'd try to be optimistic.

LURE OF THE ARCTIC

"Gentlemen," he began, "today we have a gourmet meal. Our drink will be spruce tip tea, and the main course consists of our last grizzly-mauled roasted muskrat nicely seasoned with crushed akpiks and rose hips — and a little good old N.W.T. soil for that added flavor."

"Yeah," John said. "Good old N.W.T. soil does add something to the flavor — I can't say it's anything good, but —"

"Listen!" Walter hissed.

The fire snapped in the sudden silence. Then from far away there came the low drone of a plane motor. Scrambling to their feet, each one ran to a driftwood signal.

Paul's hands shook as he struck a match and held it to the kindling at the bottom of the pile. It flickered and went out. He struck another match and shielding it from the wind he touched it to a wisp of dry moss. It burned feebly. Carefully he shook more grass and moss over the tiny flame. The sound of the plane motor was louder. He must hurry. Then suddenly the fire caught and a moment later flames were running up the center of the pile into the dry driftwood. He looked to the right. The other fires were burning too. Flames were shooting high into the air above the scraggly twenty foot, one hundred year old spruce trees. Columns of smoke drifted to the southeast.

They rushed into a clearing looking toward the north, straining their eyes to see the plane. "I see it!" Paul shouted pointing to the northeast at a red and black plane.

"It's a Piper Aztec twin engine!" Walter exclaimed. "They see us! They're changing course!"

The three waved wildly as the plane swooped low over the river. Then banking to the left, it circled Walter's downed plane two times, and again approached the camp.

"They're waving!" John shouted. "Hey! They're dropping something!"

Paul ran toward a box which had landed fifty yards upriver. John and Walter were at his heels. Tearing the box open Paul seized a paper with large handwriting on it. He read, "We have your location Cessna C GPTM. Hold on. Will send help."

The plane roared overhead once more, dipping its wings to them before returning toward the northeast. They watched it out of sight, laughing and speculating about their rescue.

"They'll send a chopper," Walter said.

"Hey, Fellows! Look in the box!" John shouted.

"Wow! Candy bars!" Paul yelled.

Ravenously they each tore open a bar and munching the unexpected treat they returned to camp. Spirits were high as they ate the roasted muskrat, now slightly black, and drank hot spruce tip tea.

"When do you think they'll send help?" John asked Walter.

"Not before tomorrow. We don't know where they are headed. Could be Inuvik — might even be Arctic

Red River or Fort McPherson." He threw more wood on the fire. "By the looks of those clouds there is snow on the way. We'd better get plenty of wood nearby."

"Oh no," Paul groaned. "Don't tell us there's going to be a storm so planes can't fly. And we're about out of meat."

"We'll hold on, like the note says," Walter replied. "They'll get to us as soon as they can. And we still have the mipku, and most of the muktuk."

The rest of the day was spent in dragging wood to camp and chopping it for the fire. As usual they kept a supply of small branches and twigs to use for kindling in case the fire went out.

The wind was blowing in fitful gusts from the north. A few snowflakes sailed by, horizontal to the ground. The three stopped work often to warm themselves at the fire, but on this day nothing could dampen their spirits. An occasional candy bar was a treat they allowed themselves.

Walter beat his hands together. "The mercury is dropping. Must be near zero."

"Maybe we should take turns staying up tonight to keep the fire going," Paul suggested.

But even though they changed shifts at the end of two hours and the fire burned furiously, the shelter was freezing cold. Part of the time all three stood by the fire, beating their hands and stamping their feet to keep circulation going. They drank quarts of spruce tip tea. Toward morning Paul remarked, "Anyway, it hasn't snowed much. If the wind lets up someone will be here today to get us." But the night seemed endless.

Then at daybreak, the snow started. Dismally they sat inside the shelter wrapped in sleeping bags, the grizzly bear rug and the two caribou hides. They went outside only long enough to throw wood on the sputtering fire. Paul thought how feeble the fire was in combating the relentless cold of the barren land.

Each time someone tended the fire they refilled the basin with packed snow so that there would be hot water to drink. Their spruce buds like the Labrador tea, were gone. Huddled together for body warmth inside the flimsy shelter, the dismal hours passed slowly.

"What will you do when we get out of here?" Walter asked Paul.

"Call my father — if he's still here. Maybe he's given us up and gone back to Toronto." Paul stared glumly into the impenetrable whiteness that obscured the river.

"How about you, John? What will you do when we get out?"

"Call my parents — and have a hamburger!"

No one spoke for a long time. Then as though he was thinking aloud Walter said, "I don't know what I'll do without my plane."

"It doesn't seem to be smashed up too bad," Paul

commented.

"I can't get it out of here."

"How about a helicopter? They'd get it out," Paul argued.

"I don't have that kind of money."

"When you get the insurance —"

"I don't have insurance."

That's Walter, Paul thought remembering the unrepaired radio and the half filled gas tank. But he had to give Walter credit for one thing. The survival box. It had saved their lives.

A sudden gust of wind snatched up a cloud of snow and whipped it around the side of the shelter into their faces. Paul brushed the snow away and stumbled outside to tend the fire which must be kept burning brightly to prevent being put out by the snow. Without the fire they'd freeze to death in their three-sided shelter. Paul stamped his numb feet.

Outside nothing looked familiar. The river was not visible through the whirling whiteness. They were encircled by a dense white wall. Against the back of the shelter the wind had piled the snow in a huge bank as high as Paul's shoulders. Turning, he rushed inside. "Hey!" he shouted. "We could build an igloo!"

Walter shook his head. "Not enough snow to make blocks."

"Come and look," Paul begged.

Reluctantly John crawled outside. "Can't we make

an igloo from that big snowbank?" Paul asked.

John's eyes lit up. "Yeah! We could dig the snow out of the inside! It would be warmer than the lean-to! Walter!"

The shovel John had made was leaning against the side of the shelter. Taking turns, they dug into the hard wind-packed snow until they had a hole inside about six feet long, four feet wide and three feet high. By late afternoon their tiny snow house was finished. The dry spruce boughs from inside the shelter were placed on the floor with a caribou hide over them for insulation from the frozen snow-covered ground. A sleeping bag was spread against each side with the tops near the low opening. The middle was left for the grizzly bear rug where Walter would sleep.

"I feel warmer," Paul commented when they had their late afternoon meal of dry mipku, a candy bar and hot water. "The exercise of digging warmed me up. My feet still feel numb though."

"We'll be warmer in the snow shelter," Walter said confidently.

Crawling inside feet first with John on the right and Paul on the left, they spread their sleeping bags flat. Walter crawled in the middle. Pulling the sleeping bags together over Walter, they held them in place with the heavy grizzly bear rug over all of them.

John put the remaining caribou hide over the low door. "I feel like one of our huskies sleeping under the snow," he chuckled.

"Will we keep the fire going?" Paul asked as he pulled the sleeping bag over his face to meet the top of his parka hood.

"When we're warm we'd better stay here," Walter said. "We still have matches."

"Matches, a little muktuk, a little mipku, three candy bars and water," Paul said. "That should be enough until they come for us."

No one answered.

"Well, shouldn't it? How long do these storms last?"

"One or two days usually. Sometimes longer," Walter replied recalling times when early fall storms had lasted five or six days. "If the weather isn't better in the morning, we'll have only one meal tomorrow. But we'll make it."

"Yeah. Some way we'll make it," John echoed Walter.

The only sound was the muffled moan of the wind through the evergreens. Soon they slept. Paul awoke during the night, surprised to find he was comfortable. John and Walter breathed deeply beside him. The next time he wakened John was peering outside under the caribou hide door. "How does it look?" he asked.

John dropped the flap. "Still snowing."

"Might as well stay here where we're warm," Walter said.

Periodically during the forenoon they peeped out,

but still the snow fell. Hunger finally drove them to get food. When they crawled outside the freezing air was like a slap in the face.

"Wow!" Paul gasped hurrying to help the others pile wood for a fire. The snow was heaped in odd shaped drifts along the edge of the trees, yet the ground in front of the shelter had been swept bare by the wind.

Soon the fire was blazing and snow was melting in the old smoke blackened basin. The wind had gone down but the snow continued to fall. After their meal of muktuk, hot water and the remaining candy bars, they sat out of the snow inside the shelter.

By mid-afternoon when the snow still continued to fall, Walter said, "No one can reach us today."

Somehow the uncomfortable hours passed until they were forced to return to the cramped quarters of the little snow house. Next morning Walter's shout wakened the others with a start. "Get up! The snow's stopped!"

Hurriedly they crawled out to unfamiliar surroundings. The river lay blanketed under a thick covering of snow. The scraggly twenty foot spruce trees looked like Christmas trees decorated with fluffy cotton. The lean-to roof was piled with a feathery eight-inch cover.

"Have to get the fire going," Walter said, "to help them find us. They can't see the Cessna with the snow on it. John, why don't you clean it off?"

After drinking hot water and gnawing a dry piece

of mipku, Walter suggested that they clean a landing spot for the helicopter. With the shovel he outlined a large triangular spot in a clearing about two hundred yards downriver from the camp.

Paul asked, "Why is it in the shape of a triangle?"

"That's a signal to pilots that means it is safe to land. We'll shovel the snow out and outline the landing spot with green spruce branches."

"That's neat!" Paul exclaimed.

John and Walter shoveled while Paul chopped and dragged branches. His ribs still were sensitive from the encounter with the grizzly, but he was determined to do his share of the work. By noon the landing spot was ready. They sat by the fire to wait with their eyes trained to the northeast and ears straining for the first sound of the chopper.

Suddenly they were up, jumping, yelling and waving as a tiny speck appeared in the sky. Shortly a blue and white helicopter with Northwest Territories Helicopter, Ltd. painted on the side set down in the center of the landing spot. Running wildly, they sprinted toward the helicopter.

The door opened and two fur clad men climbed out. "Dad!" both Paul and John shouted. For a moment fathers and sons clung to one another, speechless with happiness. Then everyone was trying to talk above the pounding of the big chopper. Paul caught his breath long enough to shout, "Who is the man with Walter?"

"His father!" Jim Douglas shouted back. "We've all been sweating it out together. He pounded Paul on the back. "You could stand a shave and hair cut, Son!"

Paul laughed. "We do look pretty scrubby, don't we?"

A fourth man was climbing down from the chopper. Paul and John couldn't believe their eyes. "Abe Gordon," Paul muttered, "The ill-tempered, surly old fellow from Tuktoyaktuk."

"What's he doing here?" John said under his breath.

The little man in the huge fur parka came toward the young men, his hand extended. "Let me be one of the first to tell you I am happy you are all right."

"Thank you," they said, perplexity showing in their faces.

Soon their few possessions were loaded into the chopper. "You travel light," Jim joked.

"We have all our clothes on," Paul said. "My sleeping bag and the slippers Grandmother Katoayak gave me are all I have."

When they were airborne John turned to his father. "Where were we?"

"On the Peel River about fifty miles south of Fort McPherson. You were found by oil geologists based in Inuvik."

"There's no way we'd have made it even if we hadn't run out of gas," Walter muttered. "Fifty miles south of Fort McPherson, and there are no more settlements south of there for many miles."

Below them the desolate land stretched as far as they could see. Gone were the lakes and streams, buried under the first big snow of winter. Soon winter roads across the frozen land and water would connect the settlements.

"When did you first know we were missing?" Paul asked his father.

"Near the end of August when you didn't come back to Tuk. We called Aklavik and learned you'd left. It was a bad time for all of us." Jim was silent a moment. "But let's not talk about that. You're all right, that's the important thing. Two days ago the geologists reported they saw signal fires and three people on the Peel River. They saw the identification letters on Walter's plane, and we were told you'd been found. None of us slept much that night." Jim's arm rested across Paul's shoulders.

"Did you call Mom and Carl — and Karen?"

"Sure did. They're planning a big party for you when you get home. I'm sure from Carl's voice that he was crying after I told him you'd been located."

"You know, Dad, I've changed my mind about Carl this summer. I've decided that taking precautions can prevent big trouble. Carl's all right."

"Good. I'm glad you feel that way. We'll start home in a day or two. You've already missed too many classes."

"Yeah. I'll probably have to wait until next term to go back to the university." Paul studied the back of Abe Gordon's head and wondered again why he had come along to rescue them.

"We're crossing the MacKenzie!" John shouted. "It's not frozen over yet!"

The blue ribbon of water stretched northward toward the Arctic Ocean. Ice fringed the shore of the big river. Soon now it would be frozen until another spring. In a short time the helicopter set down outside the modern terminal in Inuvik.

Half an hour later in the lobby of the Eskimo Inn, Abe Gordon said with some hesitation, "You fellows are wondering why I went to meet you." He coughed. "Your fathers and I have become good friends. They saved my life when my old place burned a month ago. I've never known kindness like the people of Tuk have shown me since I burned out." He paused a moment. "I thought no one liked me, and they didn't, but I know it was because my attitude was wrong. When your fathers risked their lives to drag me out of the fire, they gave me a new life as well. I've found if you give kindness and recognition, you will receive it." He looked around. "Enough seriousness. After you've had a hot bath and a shave and put on the new clothes your fathers have for you, we'll have dinner in the dining room and celebrate."

"Thanks, Mr. Gordon," the three men murmured.

LURE OF THE ARCTIC

The little man went to Walter. "Before I leave Tuk we'll send a chopper to bring your plane back."

The pilot was speechless. He grasped Abe Gordon's hand as tears filled his eyes.

Jim added, "We should also tell you that Abe stayed in Inuvik after the fire hoping you'd be found and he paid for the rescue trip. He chartered the big chopper so that Walter's father, Jack and I could go to meet you. Now before you go to shave and clean up, I'll bet you'd like a snack."

"Wow! Would we ever? A big hamburger with everything, french fries and a chocolate malted!" Paul exclaimed.

"Yeah, man!" John agreed, "and a huge mug of real tea!"

GLOSSARY

Aglu
A hole in the sea ice where seals come up to breathe

Akpiks
Bright orange-colored raspberries

Inuit
The Eskimo people

Inuk
The Eskimo man

Inutitut or **Inukitut**
The Eskimo language

Kabloona
A white person (singular)

Kabloonat
White people (plural)

Kraluarpait
Large fish

Kringak
The smoke hole

Kroak
Frozen raw fish

Kudlik
A stone lamp

Mipku
Dried strips of whale meat

Mukluks
Eskimo sealskin or caribou skin boots

Muktuk
Beluga skin and blubber preserved in oil

Nanuk
White bear or polar bear

Oopik
   Snowy owl

Sik-sik
   Arctic ground squirrel

Sila
   Weather

Tuktu
   Caribou

Ugink
   Bearded seal

Ulu
   An Eskimo woman's knife

BIBLIOGRAPHY

BOOKS

Barton, Laura Beatrice. **I Married the Klondike.** Toronto: McClelland & Stewart, Ltd., 1967.

Berry, William D. **Deneki, an Alaskan Moose.** New York: Macmillan.

Burnford, Sheila. **One Woman's Arctic.** Toronto: McClelland & Stewart, Ltd., 1973.

Crisler, Lois. **Arctic Wild.** New York: Ballantine Books, 1958.

Employment and Related Services Division, Department of Indian Affairs and Northern Development. **Northern Survival.** Ottawa, 1972.

Fredrickson, Olive A. F. **The Silence of the North.** New York: Warner Books, Inc., 1973.

Hanson, Conrad H. **Gems of the North.** Kirkland Lake, Ontario: Toburn Printing, 1979.

Hinds, Margery. **Schoolhouse in the Arctic.** Don Mills, Ontario: Geoffrey Bles, 1959.

Metayer, Maurice. **I, Nuligak.** New York: Simon & Schuster, 1971.

261

Mowat, Farley. **Lost in the Barrens.** Toronto: McClelland & Stewart, Ltd., 1973.

—. **Never Cry Wolf.** New York: Dell, 1963.

—. **Ordeal by Ice.** Toronto: McClelland & Stewart, Ltd., 1960.

—. **People of the Deer.** New York: Pyramid Books, 1951.

—. **The Polar Passion.** Toronto: McClelland & Stewart, Ltd., 1973.

Murie, Margaret E. **Two in the Far North.** New York: Ballantine, 1962.

Price, Ray. **The Howling Arctic.** Toronto: Peter Martin Associates, 1970.

—. **Yellowknife.** Toronto: Peter Martin Associates, 1967.

Pryde, Duncan. **Nunanga.** New York: Bantam, 1973.

Robbins, Brun, Singer, and Zim. **Birds of North America.** Racine, Wisconsin: Golden Press, 1966.

Smith, Francis C. **The World of the Arctic.** New York: Lippincott, 1960.

Smith, Kaj Birket. **The Eskimos.** Toronto: Ryerson Press, 1959.

Williams, Stephen Guion. **In the Middle: The Eskimo Today.** Boston: David R. Godine, 1983.

A R T I C L E S

"Aklavik, Inuvik, Tuktoyaktuk." **Northwest Territories,** First Edition.

Brockstoce, John. "Arctic Odyssey." **National Geographic,** July 1983.

Bruemmer, Fred. "Caribou." **The Beaver,** Spring 1972.

—. "Sealskin Thong." **The Beaver,** Spring 1972.

—. "Sik-sik." **The Beaver,** Spring 1972.

Chadwick, Douglas H. "Grizz: Of Men and the Great Bear." **National Geographic,** February 1986.

Ethier, Valerie Girling. "The Aurora." **The Beaver,** Summer 1968.

Fidler, Vera. "String Figures." **The Beaver,** Winter 1963.

Fisher, Mark A. "Watching Beaver." **The Beaver,** Spring 1971.

Fraser, Whit. "My Name Is Judge Berger and I Am Here to Listen to You." **Arctic in Colour,** Vol. V, No. 1.

Flyger, Vagn. "Hunters of White Whales." **The Beaver,** Winter 1965.

Fox, Audrey. "Franz Vande Velde, Polar Priest." **Arctic in Colour,** Autumn 1974.

—. "The Padre's People." **Arctic in Colour,** Autumn 1974.

Gilbert, Bil. "Canoes North — More Than Adventure." **Arctic in Colour,** Spring 1974.

Hancock, Lee. "Susie Tiktalik: The Hunt." **Arctic in Colour,** Summer 1975.

Harrington, Richard. "High Arctic Cruise." **Arctic in Colour,** Spring 1975.

Henderson, Brad. "How Northerners Play." **Arctic in Colour,** Vol. V, No. 2, 1977.

Hewitt, M. J. "A Kabloona Hunts with the Inlanders." **The Beaver,** Spring 1968.

Hohn, E. Otto. "Birds of the Muskeg." **The Beaver,** Spring 1968.

Hume, Steve. "Survive." **Arctic in Colour,** Summer 1975.

—. "The Sun Dies at Grise Fiord." **Arctic in Colour,** Summer 1972.

Inglis, George. "Fortune in Furs." **Arctic in Colour,** Spring 1975.

Joss, Annie. "Visit to a Language Camp." **Inuvaluit,** Fall 1983.

Judge, Joseph. "Peoples of the Arctic." **National Geographic,** February 1983.

Kaglik, Donald. "The Woman Who Went to the Moon." (Eskimo story.) **Inuvaluit,** Fall 1983.

McGhee, Robert. "Evacuation at Kittigaruit." **The Beaver,** Autumn 1971.

McOnie, Alan. "Summer on the Tundra." **Arctic in Colour,** Vol. V, No. 2, 1977.

Miller, Sam. "Nanook: King of the Arctic." **Arctic in Colour,** Summer 1973.

Ogle, Ed. "Canada's Arctic Today." **Arctic in Colour,** Summer 1975.

Richards, Bill. "Henry Hudson's Changing Bay." **National Geographic,** March 1982.

Robinson, William. "The Call of the Arctic." **The Beaver,** Spring 1967.

Rue, Leonard Lee. "Red Fox." **The Beaver,** Winter 1968.

Ruggles, Ruth. "Arctic Traveler." **Arctic in Colour,** Spring 1974.

Selamio, Alice. "How to Set a Fish Net." **Inuvaluit,** Fall 1983.

Sinclair, Gorde. "Only a Few Remember." **Arctic in Colour,** Spring 1974.

Sorensen, Art. "Kilaluak! Kilaluak! White Whales: A Way of Life at Tuk." **Arctic in Colour,** Summer 1972.

—. "Last of the Nomads." **Arctic in Colour,** Spring 1975.

Stevens, Robert W. "Season of the Whale." **Arctic in Colour,** Vol. V, No. 1.

Stevenson, Alex. "The Huskies." **The Beaver,** Winter 1966.

Tiktalik, Susie. "From Her Life Story." **Inuvaluit,** Spring 1982.

Verge, Pat. "Aklavik, a Future Fur Fashion Centre?" **Arctic in Colour,** Vol. VI, No. 3, 1977.

Vesilind, Priit. "Hunters of the Lost Spirit." **National Geographic,** February 1983.

—. "Arctic Sun Completes Successful Season." "Harbour Tug.) **Inuvaluit,** Fall 1983.

—. "Articles on Eskimo Life." **The Beaver,** Spring 1959.

—. "Articles on Aklavik & Inuvik." **The Beaver,** Autumn 1960.

—. "Eskimo Songs." **The Beaver,** Winter 1959.

—. "The Changing Eskimo." **The Beaver,** Summer 1962.

—. "Inuit: We Will Share Our Land." **Arctic in Colour,** Vol. IV, No. 4, 1976.

—. "Herpetology North of 60°." **The Beaver,** Summer 1971.

—. "Nanook and His Future." **Arctic in Colour,** Summer 1973.

—. "Ulu Foods." **Inuvaluit,** Spring 1982.

—. "Visit to a Whaling Camp." **Inuvaluit,** Fall 1983.

*W*ilderness *A*dventure *B*ooks
P. O. Box 968
Fowlerville, MI 48836

Please send me _____ copies of **Lure of the Arctic** at $10.95 $ _____

(\$13.95 Canadian)

(Postage will be paid by the publisher.)

Send check or money order - no cash or C.O.D.   Autographed   Yes   No

Mr./Mrs./Ms. _____

Street _____

City _____ State / Province _____ ZIP _____